RETURNING TO IRAN

RETURNING TO IRAN

Sima Nahan

URTEXT
San Francisco

Copyright ©2009 by Sima Nahan. All rights reserved. No part of this publication may be reproduced, stored in a retrieval system or transmitted in any form or by any means, electronic, mechanical, photocopying, recording, or otherwise, without the prior written permission of the copyright holder, except brief quotations used in a review.

ISBN-13: 978-0-9790573-0-4
ISBN-10: 0-9790573-0-2

Published by Urtext
San Francisco
www.urtext.us

Printed in the United States of America

Contents

Preface

Smoldering in Traffic (2005)

Returning to Iran (1986–1987)

Kashf-e Hejab (2007–2008)

Preface

Iran is a long story. It has a complicated history and an old culture. It has a seasoned people whose boldness has grown out of the tragedies they have survived. Contradictions run deep and meet their match only in perseverance. Untangling the strands of this story is as daunting an undertaking as it is compelling.

It is now thirty years since the revolution in Iran. The articles in this collection were written over the course of more than twenty of them. They are accounts of my travels in the years during which the country grew from a revolutionary state to an established regional power. What people have lived through during this time and how they have been shaped by it will undoubtedly emerge at length and from various viewpoints for many years to come. This book is an attempt to record some of those experiences and reflections.

Part I, "Smoldering in Traffic," was written after my trip to Iran in 2005, as the era of "reform" gave way to the election of Mahmoud Ahmadinejad. It is a sketch of everyday encounters and pressing questions during a few weeks of a hot Tehran summer.

Part II, "Returning to Iran," was written after my first trips home since the revolution, in 1986 and 1987. It is an account of life in the grip of internal terror and war, and the misrepresentation of Iran outside the country. Writing during a particularly dangerous time I did my best to conceal the names and identifying characteristics of people. This period came to an end with the ending of the war with Iraq and the mass executions of 1988.

Part III, "Kashf-e Hejab," 2007–2008, is a premature account of the end of another period. Here I use actual names and identifying characteristics of several individuals, drawing on their public lives and their publications in Iran—the mark of a welcome change since the early years of the revolution.

When in 1986 I first started writing about my trip I had no idea it would lead to over two decades of observations. This book began with taking notes as a reflexive response to the shock of what I was seeing in Iran. Over the years that initial shock splintered into many other complicated thoughts, but I can't say it ever wore off.

How in the world did this happen to us?

Perhaps what the non-Iranian reader will get out of this book is a glimpse into *what* has happened to Iranians after the revolution. But far too many Iranians, living inside or outside Iran, will go to their graves wondering *how* this happened to us. I certainly have no answer to the question. I am not even sure if what I am getting at is a real question, let alone whether there is an answer to it. It is just that states of bewilderment are often formulated as questions. What I can say for certain is that I am humbled by the wounded but confident people in Iran and sobered by the magnitude of their sacrifices. And regardless of what exactly happened, or how, what I have come to value over the years, perhaps above all else, are the secrets to survival: defiance, irreverence, and friendship.

Life in Iran, both above and under ground, is rich and unpredictable. My travels these years have been primarily fueled by the pleasure I derive from my connection to this life. As I go to publication with my accounts of these travels I have the lingering fear that I have jeopardized my future returns to Iran.

Sima Nahan 2009

Smoldering in Traffic

2005

Do we really deserve this?

Right after the 2005 elections an unusually hot summer descended on Tehran. After the long, cool spring, the heat wave felt particularly nasty. 42° C, 45°, 46°—people greeted each other with disbelief. Being stuck in traffic inside the mostly un-air-conditioned, sub-standard cars that make up the taxi fleets in Tehran was like having your head stuffed inside an exhaust pipe.

"We deserve this," growled an angry cab driver trapped in a gridlock. "We deserve every catastrophe that befalls us."

The most recent catastrophe, apart from the heat, was the election of Mahmoud Ahmadinejad as president. "We deserve this ape," said the cabby as his old car wailed with a downshift. A campaign ditty for Ali Akbar Hashemi Rafsanjani, the runner-up in the elections, widely forwarded on email and cell phone messages, ran something like this: "Hand in hand we vote for Akbar / Better than turning over the country to the *antar*" (the ape) and the epithet had stuck. Countering the Rafsanjani campaign ditty, the general opposition came up with: *Na Rahbar, na Akbar, na Antar*—"Neither the Leader (i.e. Khamenei), nor Akbar, nor the ape."

My trip to Iran was a personal one. It was short and heavily booked with seeing family and friends I hadn't seen since my last visit there thirteen years before. My contact with people outside my personal circle would be limited to chance encounters and random conversations. I had no plans to interview anyone or engage in political discussions, the way we used to in the early years of the revolution. But in Tehran one can no sooner get away from politics than avoid the exhaust fumes.

Politics permeates everything from family life to random encounters. Observations are acute.

On my ride from the airport the first night, the taxi driver passed on to me two widely spread rumors. The first was that Ahmadinejad used to shoot the final shots into executed prisoners at the notorious Evin Prison. The second was the speculation that he is prime assassination material. "Rafsanjani is going to do away with him," the driver said with a knowing nod. (Rafsanjani's role in the assassination of Kurdish dissidents in Germany, for one, is well documented.) When I asked him whom he voted for the driver gave a laugh. "I didn't vote," he said. "How do you choose between a murderer and an executioner?"

Elections 2005

The driving force behind the elections this year was severe dislike. People who voted for Rafsanjani detested Ahmadinejad, while Ahmadinejad supporters hated Rafsanjani with a passion. Of the two, Ali Akbar Hashemi Rafsanjani, a former president, was the better known quantity. As his spectacular defeat in the parliamentary elections of 2000 showed, however, Rafsanjani's extreme wealth and the entrenched power of his family are deeply resented. He personifies the class that has enriched itself immeasurably while subjecting the rest of the population to violence and poverty.

After the election what had remained of Rafsanjani's campaign were occasional "Hashemi 2005" bumper stickers—in English, interestingly enough—on SUVs and other upscale cars. (The wide use of "Hashemi" made many wonder if by using this name Rafsanjani wanted to distance himself from his past.) In the month before the election, local campaign headquarters had popped up in private homes in affluent neighborhoods. People who were clearly no supporters of the Islamic Republic voluntarily opened their houses to serve as campaign *setad,* where food and drink flowed and pop music blared. Posters and bumper stickers were distributed. Campaign strategy was discussed. Young women in clingy overdresses and skimpy head scarves emanated from these houses on roller blades. One approaching a car stopped in traffic stuck a "Hashemi 2005" flyer under the windshield wiper and said, "Vote for Shadmehr Aqili"—a forbidden pop singer—"This is all bullshit." A father of two teenagers remarked, "Our young people get to enjoy freedom once every four years, at election time."

The most complimentary thing I heard anyone say of Rafsanjani was: "Four years of Rafsanjani led to eight years of Khatami." To which another replied with irony, "And eight years of Khatami led to Ahmadinejad…"

"Tell your American friends," a friend of my father's told me regarding Ahmadinejad's election, "that this is what happens when a 'moderate' is succeeded by a 'reformist'." He was referring to the labels for Rafsanjani and Khatami that were made popular by American media.

Some signs of economic prosperity and political progress did appear in the Rafsanjani and Khatami years. A number of businesses flourished and a trickle of cash flowed down. Attempts were made to adjust government salaries for inflation and to hold the devaluation of the currency in check. Apart from a spurt of gruesome murders of writers and intellectuals, known as the "chain murders," and the particularly barbaric suppression of student dissent, extremist violence was reduced. Censorship was relaxed periodically. There was more toleration of elementary civil liberties such as wearing makeup and listening to popular music. Some attributed this toleration to Khatami's efforts to implement the constitution and establish the rule of law.

But Ahmadinejad addressed urgent needs that were not touched by the tentative and cosmetic improvements of the past decade. While Rafsanjani banked on the vote of upscale youth hungry for civil liberties and disposable income, Ahmadinejad spoke to people living in unrelenting poverty. As even the middle class was forced to take on second and third jobs to afford skyrocketing rents and living expenses, anger against the status quo built up. Rafsanjani symbolized the corruption that stifled real economic growth. (Could he have forgotten that the charge of corruption against the Shah's regime was its kiss of death?)

Ahmadinejad's promises for fighting corruption, solving housing problems, creating new jobs, and bringing down prices appealed to a wide spectrum of the population. His concrete plans, however, were not known. Soon after the election he said that he was going to surprise everyone. Rumor had it that during his campaign he had promised to "staple" the slipping veils of young women to their foreheads. After the campaign he was said to have retracted: "There are other priorities…"

As nobody hangs on anybody's words in Iran, the general attitude was not to comb Ahmadinejad's words for meaning but to wait and see. While people waited, large financial and business transactions were put on indefinite hold. The stock market barely functioned. At some point the new president said that he was going to replace eighty percent of those in managerial positions in the government. This had a significant effect on the functioning of government officials. At the foreign ministry, more than once I overheard this piece of advice offered to people by the authorities: "Do it now while we're here. There's no telling what will happen in six months…"

Ahmadinejad's inflammatory discourse on restoring the values of the revolution, including violent measures against infringements of religious decree, had appeal for hardliners who, after all, would be the human resource for implementing his plans. While the country waited, a great many people had misgivings about any plans that would be carried out by hardliners with free recourse to violence. People worried that implementing rent control, for instance, really meant confiscation of property. In the past, battling high prices had meant unleashing thugs on merchants and looting stores. A return to this brand of thuggery and lawlessness was dreaded—not to mention that in the past this course of action had resulted in shopkeepers taking merchandise off their shelves and offering them under the table at jacked-up prices.

The disbelief and dread felt by Ahmadinejad's opposition notwithstanding, it is undeniable that millions of people voted for him. Charges of coercion and cheating in the election process abound, but even if some of the charges are justified, in the end that is just quibbling. Ahmadinejad has considerable popular support. When I heard the result of the elections just before going to Iran, I thought it was indicative of some kind of mass hysteria. But in Iran, I heard some perfectly calm accounts of why he was elected. "Ahmadinejad is an honest man," his supporters said. "He lives modestly." "He doesn't steal." "He will stop corruption." I would venture that he is focused and unflinching, with a certain degree of eloquence. When he was asked whether he thought his appearance was presidential enough, he answered that he's satisfied to look like a servant of the country.

While many people voted for Rafsanjani out of fear of the hardliners but without any real love of their own candidate, most Ahmadinejad supporters not only hated Rafsanjani but liked their own candidate. What remained of Ahmadinejad's campaign after the election were not slick posters and bumper stickers in English; they were handwritten scribbles on walls: "Dr. Ahmadinejad." While his antagonists gleefully repeated jokes about his looks, size, and advanced degree, his supporters found him "a man of the people." A television clip showed a scruffy-looking little boy hurrying somewhere. "Where are you running to?" he was asked. "To congratulate my neighbor," he said. "He was elected president."

Who voted for Ahmadinejad?

I had not expected to find Ahmadinejad supporters among my own acquaintances. At the home of some friends of my mother I nearly choked when the young hostess said sweetly, "I almost called you in the U.S. to ask you to vote for Dr. Ahmadinejad."

We were visiting the family in their small but cheerfully furnished and electronically equipped apartment. This was a traditional Iranian family, highly observant of form (five main courses for three guests, accompanied by a multitude of elaborate side dishes) and pious (the woman veiled by conviction, the conversation running to the impossibility of explaining to non-Shiites the significance of Hazrat-e Abolfazl). The bedroom of the three-year old son was crammed with the latest Disney toys and videos. On his desk was a more powerful and better-equipped computer than I use, with Internet access and lots of children's software. The wife was a warm-hearted special education teacher with high moral standards. (Her mother had until recently been a "women's affairs" advisor to an old-time hardliner who had also run for election this year.) The husband was a graphic artist and an award-winning photographer, his bookshelves packed with art books. He was a two-time voter for Khatami, but the wife had not voted for Khatami on his second term. While husband and wife were both religious, the husband seemed altogether more liberal than his wife.

"I did not vote," I said in response to her comment about calling us. "I support neither Ahmadinejad nor Rafsanjani."

And I could not help adding: "I am not religious—quite, quite secular, in fact."

That being established to mutual respect, we discussed Ahmadinejad. As it turned out, the husband and wife's candidate in the first round of elections was not the newcomer Ahmadinejad but an old hardliner. In the second round, however, out of severe dislike for Rafsanjani they had voted for Ahmadinejad. "Rafsanjani had already proved himself to be corrupt," the wife said, "so it was easier to give benefit of the doubt to a new candidate." She added: "And he's not inexperienced. He's already been governor of Semnan and mayor of Tehran."

I asked about Ahmadinejad's background at Evin. "Rumors, Rafsanjani propaganda..." she said. "Dr. Ahmadinejad was a professor before he became governor and mayor. Besides, back then"—the executions he is accused of were in the 1980s—"he was nobody to have a job like that." I thought that was odd, as if firing last shots was a coveted position reserved for the elite. Everyone knew, for instance, that one of the ways in which the *tavvabs,* the "repentant" prisoners, proved their loyalty to the Islamic Republic was to volunteer to fire those notorious shots. That particular act seems to have been a way to prove oneself. But I did not push the issue with my hosts.

"Ahmadinejad has plans to develop the country in a way that benefits society," she said. "And he is just the kind to get rid of corruption. He is an honest man. He is strong and principled. He is not compromising." The latter, of course, was exactly what was least reassuring to the rest of us. "Just wait and see," she said.

A second surprise Ahmadinejad supporter was Akram, whom my extended family has known for nearly thirty years. She started by giving my mother and aunts massages and manicures and became a family friend. She is quite a woman. As a single mother she raised her son with hard work through the very difficult years of revolution and war. She is a strong and athletic woman who has climbed the 18,000-foot Mount

Damavand several times. Her passion is mountaineering and, as a woman, she is a novelty and quite popular in the predominantly male climbing community. Over the years she has picked her boyfriends by testing their endurance in the mountains first. She tells funny stories of how she wears down lightweight men who can't keep up with her.

Akram is no lightweight in anything she does. In the early years of the revolution, at a memorial service for her brother who was martyred in the war with Iraq, a fleet of mourning ladies, courtesy of the government, had showed up scratching their faces and chanting: "This flower was withered in the path of the Leader." Even in those fearful days Akram had not been intimidated. "He died for his country, not the Leader," she had said, throwing the ladies out and threatening to break their necks if they returned. Her most recent confrontation was with a neighbor who insisted on leaving the outside light on during the night. The light shone in Akram's bedroom and kept her awake. The neighbor who was adamant about having it her way was a *basij*—militia—group leader and confident of her own connections (her husband merely drove a cab and could not be counted on for clout). Altercations between the two women followed, during one of which the *basiji* woman pulled a knife on Akram. Akram pressed charges and succeeded in taking her to court. After the court hearing (which was favorable to her) Akram went home and upturned all the neighbor's flowerpots into the bargain. "I don't buy any of that basij stuff," she said.

I was shocked to hear that Akram had voted for Ahmadinejad. "But you're no supporter of the Islamic Republic," I objected. "I hate the mullahs," she said, "but he's not one of them. He's one of us. He is a man of the people. And he's promised to solve our housing problem."

For decades now Akram has lived in a perpetual housing crisis, moving from apartment to apartment, barely able to pay the rent and the huge deposits. Her work takes her to all kinds of affluent houses. "I hate it that I have to work so hard when these rich people live in posh towers and make money building and selling them. Ahmadinejad is going to put a stop to all that."

One morning Akram cancelled a trip to Behesht-e Zahra, the huge cemetery of Tehran, to come see us. She showed up with a plate of *nazri* halva. It is common to make a *nazr*, a sort of vow, to distribute halva at the cemetery in memory of a departed loved one. I asked whom the halva was for. "Don't you know the anniversary of whose death it is today?" she asked with affront. I had no idea. "The Shah," she said. "May his grave be showered in light."

"I liked the Shah personally and I like Ahmadinejad personally," she said. And to seal the conversation she added, "I even like the way Ahmadinejad looks."

Another interesting supporter of the new president was a young taxi driver I rode with one evening. He was eager to initiate a conversation. "Excuse me, *khanom*," he said, "What is the best way to learn English?"

As I was searching for suggestions that would be available to him, he asked if I thought the "Oxford" books and tapes were any good. I did not know what books he was talking about, but I said, "Yes, probably." He asked if it was true that from these books you learn English with a "literary accent." I said that you probably learned English with a British accent. Then he asked if I thought TOEFL classes were better. I said that as far as I knew TOEFL was a test for getting into American colleges and perhaps a language class less focused on passing a particular exam would be better. He did not know what TOEFL was.

By this time I had a chance to check him out a little. He was very young and new to Tehran from Khuzestan. He still didn't know the city very well and was the only driver I saw who had a map handy. I asked if he went to school. "I used to be a university student," he said, "but I had to drop out for medical reasons."

"Why are our youth deceived by the mirage of the west?" he then asked just as abruptly as he had asked about learning

English. "Mirage of the west" sounded like a stock phrase that he had picked up somewhere. "Why do they only think about clothes and possessions?" he asked. I said that there are empty-headed youth in every society, and sensing a bit of hostility toward "westernized" youth I added that nevertheless it is not good for anyone to force his own values on others.

"Yes, that's what I always told them," he said. "We should allow them to do what they want, I used to say. We should not harass them."

His use of "we" was interesting. I wondered if he was or had been a basiji and, as such, a quota student at the university from which he had dropped out. I brought the conversation back to learning English and asked if he wished to go abroad to study. "No, no," he said, "all our young people who go abroad learn bad things. They don't study and they don't come back." I said that a lot of them did study and would come back if there were jobs for them. "Yes, they should come back," he agreed, forgetting his earlier hostile tone. "Dr. Ahmadinejad will create jobs for them." His mind was all over the place.

Surprisingly, this intellectually struggling young man had more concrete ideas of what Ahmadinejad was going to do than more educated and experienced supporters I talked to. Commenting about the traffic problem, he said that the new president had some good plans. "There are many companies headquartered in Tehran whose business is really in other parts of Iran," he said. "Dr. Ahmadinejad will send all these companies back to the provinces where they do their business." He did not use the word "decentralization" but tried to explain it to me as one of the president's plans. "You see," he said, "there is no agriculture in Tehran. Why should the ministry of agriculture be in Tehran? If some of the companies and government ministries move to different provinces, the population and traffic will be reduced in Tehran."

He took it a step further. "There are too many people working in the government anyway. In Scotland, the ministry of agriculture has only forty-one employees. The rest of the work is done by outside companies." Small government, privatization, outsourcing! How in the world did these ideas creep into the revolutionary discourse of the new president, and from there to supporters such as this young man? And where did the forty-one employees of the ministry of agriculture in Scotland come from? Clearly someone was stimulating the minds of young people like this driver.

I did not leave him unchallenged, however. I explained that cutting down government agencies and giving out the work to private companies is called privatization. I told him it can eventually cost the government more money and hurt the workers as the companies increase their profit. I also said that as far as I knew, Rafsanjani was the champion for privatization; Ahmadinejad was supposed to protect people's interest, not to further the cause of money-making companies. "That's not good," he agreed with me. "It's not good at all if companies make money off the government. That comes out of the budget of the country." Had his views not flip-flopped a number of times already I would have flattered myself that I had made him think. Nevertheless, I had not met anyone so hungry for education as this young driver—hungry for education at best, and at worst, at the bid and call of political cynicism. He would have probably pulled the car over and talked all night.

When we got out of the taxi I gave him a good tip. He refused it with the usual ceremony and I pressed it on him with due ceremony. I told him that his time was worth a lot more than this and that he should go back to school. He accepted shyly and beamed a smile at me as he drove off.

Greater Tehran

Since my last visit in 1992 Tehran had changed almost unrecognizably. Back then the country was still *jang-zadeh*—war-stricken. The walls were plastered with war propaganda and death-to-America slogans. Food and consumer goods were in short supply. It was long enough after the revolution that cars and buildings had aged, unmaintained. New buildings were scarce and the best homes were still the old ones, tucked away inside leafy gardens. Apart from few and far-between billboards advertising rice-cookers and blenders, advertising was refreshingly absent.

Now, commercial goods are abundant at hefty prices. Billboard advertising appears all over the new highways and throughways that crisscross the city, built to relieve traffic. The stop-and-go traffic on even the newest and widest roads creates an ideal captive audience. The advertising is mostly for electronic and communication gadgets, kitchen appliances, and prep schools to increase chances of getting admitted to good universities, but there is even some advertising for luxury goods—Swiss watches, for instance. New, air-conditioned cars with windows tightly rolled up are not rare sights in the affluent parts of town any more.

The number of virulent revolutionary slogans and murals has somewhat diminished, except for those celebrating individual martyrs or martyrdom itself. One gigantic mural shows a woman holding a baby, both of them wearing white headbands signifying readiness for martyrdom. "We love our children but we love martyrdom more," it says. Many slogans nowadays run to the moralistic, addressing the youth in the old *nasihat* tradition: "We must be truthful." "We must be diligent." "We must read fifteen minutes every night."

I only saw overt anti-American slogans on the walls of the "den of spies," the old American embassy compound. Without fanfare, however, there was advertising for American companies. Calvin Klein and Head and Shoulders were there. So was Caterpillar, occupying a clean new building marked openly with the name of the company. A cab driver told me that it sold spare parts through the Iranian *Tejarat* bank. On the other hand, it was amusing to see that the street named after Bobby Sands in the early days of the revolution had not been changed to a martyr's name like so many others.

Before the revolution the population of Tehran was 2.5 million. Now it is estimated at 12 million at least. The city has expanded in every direction, but mainly to the north and the south, to become "Greater Tehran"—*Tehran-e Bozorg*. The general vicinity of the great bazaar—the old "downtown" where the central bank, main post office, a number of ministries and museums, and many other significant establishments are still located—is now pretty much central. Outside government buildings, rows of scribes still sit on the ledge of the water canals with ancient typewriters, or simply writing tablets and pens, in their laps. This is, in fact, the least changed part of town, since many old buildings in various stages of dilapidation are under the "protection" of the National Heritage Institute. Decrepit as much of the area and many of the buildings are, something of the old beauty and architectural integrity still remains.

I visited the house of an old teacher and friend of my father in Pamenar, not too far from the bazaar. His exquisite 150-year-old house is protected as part of the country's national heritage. It is a gem indeed even if he cannot afford to fix the crumbling walls and leaking plumbing. The secluded courtyard with the blue-tiled pool and fountain in the middle is surprisingly quiet. We plucked ripe figs from the trees and rinsed them in the pool. The sound of the rustling leaves and trickling water was somehow undisturbed by street noise. Inside, the rooms were airy and bright and quite tolerable without air conditioning. The basement was positively cool, with sunlight streaming in through the wooden window lattices. My father's teacher recounted a memory of Ahmad Shah stopping by in his splendid carriage and asking whom the house was built for. "Your grandfather's physician," he was told. That was nearly a century ago. It is the kind of house where it is possible, and tempting, to wipe contemporary Tehran out of one's consciousness.

The city expands far to the south with satellite towns, partly shantytowns, partly planned neighborhoods. By far the majority of the new population of the city—mostly migrants from villages but also Afghan and Arab refugees—has settled here, though not all the satellite towns are officially part of Greater Tehran. But this is not the site of the great construction boom. The lucrative development is going on in the more affluent north where endless rows of high-rise towers stretch far up into the outskirts of the Alborz range. These are enormous residential and commercial buildings—many with rooftop helicopter pads—whose nonstop construction, given the dire economic condition of the country, defies all logic. This real estate development has driven housing prices through the roof for the rest of the population. Karbaschi, a former mayor who was popular on account of planting trees and instituting good garbage collection, relaxed zoning restrictions and sold building rights to developers against all considerations of safety and feasibility. Succeeding mayors seem to have followed suit.

Old narrow alleys that developed out of dirt foot paths in what used to be villages in northern Tehran are now crammed with cars. Not too long ago it was the weary donkeys or *chamoush* mules of peddlers that slowed traffic for the few neighborhood cars. Now the donkeys and mules have been replaced by pickup trucks piled high with melons and the singsong cries of the peddlers have given way to amplified bullhorns. The day after my arrival I assumed that cries on loudspeakers in the distance were chants or propaganda blared from some mosque, as in the early days of the revolution, but as the sound traveled nearer I was pleasantly surprised that it belonged to peddlers selling tomatoes and cucumbers, or buying used clothes and household knick-knacks. On an unusually quiet street one day I heard a young man on an accordion, singing the title song from an old movie *Soltan-e Qalbha*—Sultan of Hearts. I smiled at him sweetly as he passed by and he gave me a dirty look. Later I was told that the singer was not being quaint—he was panhandling.

Now these tight and crooked streets have to accommodate not only the neighborhood population explosion but also the cars avoiding the stop-and-go traffic of major streets. The savvier the driver, the better he or she knows how to zigzag through them. But these tiny alleys still have some of their old charm. Small produce and grocery stores are still strung with colored lights at night. The entrance to old mosques and bath houses are framed with red bricks and blue tiles chipped with age and rounded on the edges. Mechanics still work on ancient cars poking out of small garages as idle young men look on.

In the unlikeliest upscale neighborhoods, militia recruitment centers are announced with gigantic banners: "The sisters' basij of Niavaran accepts members." Here and there a new mosque with a prefabricated facade is stuffed into a tight corner. And on each side of the old or reconverted buildings a tower is going up, surrounded by piles of dirt, lumber, and concrete.

Old houses with big gardens, now called "villas," are knocked down and replaced by high-rises. The doorbells of old villas are rung many times daily with propositions from developers. Flyers are left at the door even more often. The standard practice is that the villa owner provides the land and the developer the investment, a tower goes up, and the original owner gets one or more units. Because of the cost and hassle of maintaining a big house and garden many villa owners welcome the tradeoff.

Inside the remaining villas the beautiful old trees are

covered with dust from the surrounding construction. Still, they maintain something of the cool and fragrant delight of the southern slopes of the Alborz. At a friend's old house in Velenjak, the swimming pool was filled with icy cold well water and shaded by enormous trees. We warmed up in the ancient cedar sauna before jumping in. We floated on the water and ate mulberries that had fallen in the pool. They were a little dusty.

Getting acquainted

As population grows and construction explodes, traffic chokes the city. New, domestically assembled cars stream into the streets daily, while no old cars running on leaded gasoline are retired. Delivery services are widely used. Anything from groceries and restaurant food to haircuts and beauty services are delivered to doors in the affluent parts of town. And of course the number of taxis on the streets, both official and unofficial, increases daily.

There are two kinds of cabs in Tehran, those who take you door to door and those you hail for specific distances as you incrementally approach your destination. The latter you share with other passengers, generally three in the back seat and one or two in the front. I noticed a change in the tenor of conversations in these taxis. In the early days of the revolution and war, conversation was much livelier. Back then, these random assemblies were used by drivers and passengers to vent anger at the way things were. Inevitably someone would find opportunity to hiss the old threat that someday a mullah would hang from every *chenar* tree on former Pahlavi Avenue. People seemed to get energized by taking strangers into political confidence and to derive solace from the camaraderie. Now, these accidental groups don't quite gel. Cab rides are much quieter. Even though people speak freely and with more sophistication when they have a chance, the sense of urgency to connect and communicate with strangers has somewhat faded. Oddly, there used to be a sense of hope in the dark days of revolution and war; now the mood is exhausted and depressed. Political views are no longer black and white, for and against, us and them. Nevertheless it is taken for granted that with the exception of a very small group of people everyone wants change.

I found the door-to-door *agence* cabs more conducive to conversation. It is a rare driver that avoids a conversation and most are eager to engage in elaborate discussions. The stop and go traffic creates ample opportunity for the driver and passenger to make each other's acquaintance. At the end of a long trip you sometimes regret breaking away from the talk and there are times when the driver just pulls over and you continue talking, saying goodbye eventually with reluctance. Some give you their cards so you can call them directly (not through the agency that gets a cut of their fare) if you need a car and driver for a whole day. The social, professional, and educational background of these drivers is staggeringly diverse. Half the male population of Tehran seems to have to resort to driving these cabs at one time or another, either as a main or supplemental form of income. The drivers may be old or young, college graduates or barely literate, and with any imaginable background. I rode with retired air force pilots, former factory owners, teachers, civil servants, engineers, and a great many jack-of-all-trades. I heard that there are even physicians who at one point or another resort to driving cabs.

The plurality of views and convictions among these men was eye-opening. Among them were supporters of Khatami, Ahmadinejad, Rafsanjani, the Shah, as well as bitter antagonists of all of them. There were those with combination views: pro-Khomeini but anti-Islamic Republic (the "revolution went wrong" philosophy); pro-Reza Shah but anti-Mohammad Reza Shah ("the father had guts, the son didn't"); pro-Khatami and also pro-Ahmadinejad ("one couldn't effect change, the other will"); and any number of less articulate or even more contradictory combinations. But ultimately these men's personal thoughts and experiences were most interesting, and with these they were characteristically open and forthcoming.

One hot day our driver apologized for needing to pull over for a minute to cool off. He drank from his flask of cold water and rested a bit in the shade. He explained that he is a *janbaz* (injured war veteran) still suffering from the effects of mustard gas on his lungs and skin. The heat brings on breathing difficulties. (*Janbaz*, "one who risks his life," is a relatively new official term—an improved replacement for the old *shahid-e zendeh*, "living martyr.") The janbaz are ranked according to injury: 25 percent disability is the lowest rank qualifying for benefits. But our driver, 25-percent-janbaz with 122 months of service, was not qualified for benefits because he was a retired army officer with a pension. Janbaz benefits are reserved for militia (*basij*) members who do not have a retirement. With pensions far from enough to support a family, many non-basij war veterans resort to driving cabs. This driver had also suffered an injury to his leg from a landmine, a relatively minor injury as those go. I told him that a few years back I had learned that the Islamic Republic does not allow aid from international organizations to victims of landmines. "Don't believe those organizations," he told me. "Their money comes from the companies that make the landmines." He said that there are still plenty of antipersonnel and anti-tank landmines left in the fields in Khuzestan, blowing up farmers and tractors. "Let them come and clear the fields instead of distributing prosthetics—those we can make ourselves."

Another 25-percent-janbaz, with 82 months of service at the front and a leg injury, said that he had decided not to retire from military service. He was a powerfully built and tightly wound man who could barely fit in the driver's seat. He said that he was in a special forces unit—"like the American Green Berets," he explained—and that for him retirement would be death, although he was feeling the effects of his age and injury. "I drive a cab because I need money, but I'm a warrior, not a taxi driver," he said. I asked whether the Islamic Republic was not afraid of a coup d'état by disaffected people like him in the armed forces. "Maybe," was all he said. (Some say that the election of the new president will eventually reveal itself as the military coup that it is—a coup by the corps of revolutionary guards and not the armed forces.) I felt his reluctance and pressed: "Some people say a military coup is the only alternative to this regime—some even fantasize about a coup by the supporters of Reza Pahlavi—what do you think?" He fidgeted in his seat, clearly uneasy about discussing this. "Look," he finally said. "We are mercenaries. We need a strong leader."

Some drivers pass on interesting information. One driver who spoke some English told me that before the elections a group of foreign journalists hired him to drive them around. He said that they met with people in high positions for interviews and were also interested in the political prisoners at Evin. I asked if he remembered the names of the newspapers. He named some American ones. "But it was strange," he said. "They were constantly on the phone with their editors taking directions about whom to talk to and what to ask. I thought journalists were free in America."

I had a particularly interesting long talk with one driver whose front seat was covered with newspapers and books. He occasionally pulled one out to demonstrate a point. He was a Khatami supporter and called him Iran's greatest statesman after Mosaddeq (the prime minister who nationalized oil in 1953 and was ousted through a joint US/British coup). "Mosaddeq's motto was 'educated nation, powerful government,' but Khatami's was 'educated nation, powerful *country*,'" he said. "Khatami was working not just to build a government competent to rule but a nation competent to rule itself." He pointed to the many publications on the seat next to him. "When Khatami became president we only had two newspapers. During his tenure the hardliners forced the closing down of over ninety publications. That means hundreds were given permission to publish."

I asked him whether he thought it was likely that the U.S. would attack Iran. He laughed. "This is all posturing. Each time the wheeling and dealing behind the scenes comes to an impasse one side comes out with a bluff. At this point it's the Americans who are doing most of the bluffing." I jokingly asked if he agreed with Khomeini's famous words: "America cannot do a damn thing." "No, not exactly," he said. "They can do a lot of damned things, but their military hands are tied right now. They cannot possibly pull off another occupation like in Iraq, but why would they want to do that in the first place? This regime has a lot of use for them—in fact, the hostility is useful for both sides. One keeps the other in power." This analysis is quite common in Iran—the U.S., Israel, and the Islamists are seen as mutually dependent and soul mates in brutality and deceit. So what is the concrete bargaining chip of the Islamic Republic vis-à-vis the Americans, I wanted to know. "To dominate the region the U.S. does not need actual military presence everywhere. It can have intelligence presence at much less cost," he said. "The Islamic Republic can provide that—it's already sitting on a lot of intelligence. We can be the eye and ear of the Americans."

"But America is not our immediate problem," he continued. "Poverty is." He pulled out a magazine to show me an estimate that between eleven and twenty-two million Iranians live below the poverty line. "That's why people voted for Ahmadinejad. That's why they voted for Qalibaf who outright promised 50,000 tomans for every vote." We laughed about the effects of inflation: Back during the revolution, the Islamists promised that 100-toman bills—the oil money the Shah pocketed, it was explained—would be distributed door to door after the Shah was gone. (A young woman from Mashhad told me of her conversation with an old gardener of her family who was going to vote for Qalibaf. She mimicked the gardener's Sabzevari accent: "100,000 tomans for me and my wife and another 100,000 for my son and his wife, that's 200,000 tomans right there." She laughed, "I told him, *Amu Jan*, see how good it is that women have the right to vote?")

A few times this driver referred to his lack of formal education. I told him that I thought he was more informed and well read that many educated intellectuals. "Never underestimate our intellectuals," he said. "It is their work and sacrifice that has educated people like me. They have paid a high price. We owe them a great deal."

And in the thick of the politics, oppression, and high general anxiety, there were those self-composed individuals who maintained a cheerful sanity that was almost shocking. I rode with one driver who would not speak a harsh word about anyone. He spoke with equal respect of the Shah, Khomeini, and everyone else. He made measured comments about moderation and public participation. (I saw murals extolling "public participation" in elections.) I wondered if, as a truly polite gentleman, that was his way of avoiding a conversation with me.

Twice I rode with a driver in his mid-thirties who was only interested in talking about his daughter. "When she was three my wife noticed that there was a clicking sound in her knee joints. She wanted to take her to the doctor but I said it was not necessary. I told her all she needed was lots of full-fat milk and exercise," he said. "When I was a child I had the same problem and it was cured by the milk they gave to school children during the Shah's time. Every day when I go home I take my daughter a bottle of high fat milk and sit with her until she drinks it all. I work out every day with weights myself, and she watches and copies me lifting bean cans. I've also enrolled her in gymnastics class and now you should see her run and jump on the parallel bars! No more popping knee caps…"

The rumor mill

Word of mouth still plays an important role in Tehran. People rely on it for many things—from finding the best doctors or schools or the way to get something done, to receiving and passing on news that does not make it to the media. A taxi driver, for instance, will carry a first-hand account of the vigil in front of Tehran University for the student Akbar Mohammadi who is on hunger strike at Evin. [He died in prison in September, 2006.] The next day you can learn of a women's demonstration in front of the university. If you ask, you will be informed.

Rumors are the natural offspring of word-of-mouth. They can be piercingly true or disappointingly false. Driving through the town, friends and drivers identify mega tower after mega tower belonging to Rafsanjani's family members or other high-ranking mullahs. The rumor is that it is the ruling clergy that have most heavily invested in the construction boom and it is the construction industry that is keeping the economy somewhat afloat. There is probably some truth to that. Other rumors, while indicative of something that is hard to articulate, are merely amusing. I heard from a few different cab drivers that the reason Condoleeza Rice is fixated on Iran—*be Iran gir dadeh*—is because an Iranian man with whom she had been involved had jilted her. "It's all over the foreign presses," I was told.

The rumors against Ahmadinejad seemed to merit particular attention, however. Did this guy really execute people in the prisons? Is it possible to verify these kinds of charges? I put these questions to many people. One gentleman whose social and professional background made him a plausible source thought it was possible to find out the truth. He said that while the gates of Evin are impenetrably shut to outsiders, there are insiders in possession of all kinds of documents and evidence. "You'd be surprised how much video footage exists of what has gone on inside," he said. He mentioned the trials that were held inside the prisons and the information that was exchanged during them. I had seen an early BBC documentary about two gay men who were subsequently executed. As this gentleman said, there was considerable trial footage. It is reassuring to think that someday the truth will be known.

A couple of times I played devil's advocate with Ahmadinejad supporters who despised Rafsanjani. I said that if the charge against Ahmadinejad is just a malicious rumor, then so is Rafsanjani's legendary wealth. After all, I reminded them, the Shah's wealth was also greatly exaggerated. The bottom line response was that the rumors against Rafsanjani, by virtue of having been in circulation longer, were more true than the ones against the new president.

Just for the fun of it, I conducted an informal poll on the reliability of word-of-mouth. I asked a number of cab drivers—from very different backgrounds, remember—about where to find the best traditional ice cream and *faloudeh* in town. In the end the field narrowed down to two stores, corresponding to the choices of my friends and passing my own taste test. The same thing happened with the best pastry shops. Applying the same poll-taking to the rumors against Rafsanjani and Ahmadinejad, problematic as it is, did also yield something of a consensus. Setting aside bitterly partisan responses, it was generally agreed that there was something to the rumors against both of them, the exact truth of which cannot yet be determined.

But there was one case in which I could not reach any conclusions from the rumors. The fate and condition of Akbar Ganji, the highest-profile political prisoner at Evin, remained unknowable. [He was released in May, 2006.] Everyday there was a new rumor: "He broke his hunger strike." "He didn't, but he's dying." "He is put on IV." "He is dead." "He is at Milad Hospital." "He was taken back to Evin." There was a rumor that Shirin Ebadi had tried to see him by sneaking inside the hospital from the roof. It was said that Said Mortazavi, the independently operating head of the judiciary and chief public prosecutor in Tehran, had set up office at the hospital to personally monitor Ganji's every breath and every word. "His hunger strike has made it easier for us," Mortazavi had allegedly said. "It is better for him to die in the hospital than in prison." He was probably referring to various human rights groups making a nuisance of themselves if Ganji died in prison.

From the balcony of a friend's house we had a good view of Milad, one of the best-equipped hospitals in the city. This is a new and attractive white building with green-tinted windows. One maximum security top floor is entirely devoted to victims of Evin and other prisons. The crushed body of Zahra Kazemi, the Iranian-Canadian journalist who was raped and beaten into a coma when caught photographing and interviewing families of prisoners outside Evin, was brought to this hospital two years ago. She died there. [Mortazavi is personally implicated in the beating of Kazemi. He was appointed to head the Iranian delegation to the UN Human Rights Council in June 2006.] We tried to imagine what was going on inside as we looked. A close relative of Abbas Amir Entezam, another high-profile and longstanding political prisoner, said that Amir Entezam guesses that Ganji was brought to Milad for knee surgery. The menisci in the knees apparently disintegrate after long periods of hunger strike and inactivity. (Amir Entezam, jailed for seventeen years and in and out of prison for twenty-seven, should know.) Meanwhile Ganji was to have released a new statement: "Khamenei must go"—a pointed echo of Khomeini's famous "The Shah must go." Why would Mortazavi worry about Ganji's knees, we wondered.

As of this writing the fate of Ganji—whether he's dead or alive—is not known. On this one, the rumor mill has both spun out of control and come to a stop.

Young people

For an encore at an outdoor concert at Niavaran Palace, the singer sang a popular song, "Tehran Nights." The balmy night with a full moon, the majestic old trees of the garden, and the twinkling lights of the elegant old palace of Ahmad Shah reverberated with the song's lyrics: "Tehran nights, concealing many melodies…" This is an old song whose revival has reached Iran via the exiled Iranian community in Los Angeles. It evokes not just the nostalgia of the exiled community but the lamentation for stolen life shared by Iranians inside and outside the border. It is the stealing of *their* lives that young people now resist with a vengeance. This resistance has given the old "concealed melodies" of Tehran nights an increasingly shrill edge.

The daytime activity of most young people—from teens to early twenties—is school. The relatively new phenomenon of "nonprofit schools" (no one was able to explain to me what makes these schools with their exorbitant tuitions "nonprofit") absorbs young people in afterschool and summer programs as well as the regular academic-year session. Some of these schools provide college-level technical training. Many prepare high school students for passing the dauntingly difficult country-wide entrance exam, the *concours,* to good universities. One day I was handed a flyer advertising one of these preparatory schools listing the names of instructors and the students who had been accepted in first rate universities in last year's concours. The instructors were listed only by last name, but the full names of the students revealed that a solid majority were women. I had heard that now sixty percent of university students are women, but if this flyer was any indication, the ratio is much higher. Of the students listed, in electrical engineering 4 out of 7 were female, in architecture 5 out of 6, in management 14 out of 21, and in law 15 out of 16. In medicine and computer engineering the ratio was fifty-fifty, and in mechanical engineering and dentistry all the accepted students were female.

(On a different track, two huge billboards on Sadr Highway advertise the Cultural/Scientific Institute of Koran Students—*Mo'asseseh-ye Farhangi Elmi-ye Qoran Pazhuhan*—where bachelor's degrees are awarded upon the cover-to-cover memorization of the Koran: "No high school diploma necessary.")

What is not lost on young people, however, even to those working hard to get into good schools, is that the future awaiting them is far from appealing. Jobs are few and the rewards hardly satisfying. Education borders on useless. Depression and suicide rates are high. Drugs are widely available. A number of taxi drivers told me that groups of young people hire cabs to drive them around while they freebase in the backseat. The drug most commonly used is called *shisheh*—glass—which was described as little piles of cloudy crystals. No one I talked to knew what exactly it was.

Against this backdrop young people stake their claim to having a life. Taking control of their appearance is an obsession. The overdress-qua-veil that young women wear—their *dogmeh-paroun* (button-popping) *manteau*—is cropped and pinched not just to reveal but exaggerate every curve. The scarves on their heads are little more than loose, wide headbands. Eyebrows are waxed and tattooed into severe black lines. Makeup is excessive and grotesque. Boys run the gamut from shaved heads and tattoos to retro pompadours and tight shirts. Both boys and girls openly flaunt noses bandaged from plastic surgery.

Cruising the streets and shopping malls are their chief public activity. Carloads of shrieking kids race each other on the highways, swigging and waving bottles. Groups of young guys hover in juice shops scrutinizing every young woman with predatory gaze. One night, caught in the middle of a three-lane traffic jam, I felt the piercing glance of a carful of young men to our right. A flood of unadulterated testosterone shot right through our car to the one on our left, where a group of painted young ladies looked straight ahead in studied nonchalance.

Parks are widely used in Tehran at nights. Everyone, from little children to old people, come to cool off and hang out. At the children's area of a park one night my son gravitated to a puppy accompanying a very young couple. While he was busy with the puppy—a male dog named Jennifer—the young woman and I chatted. She was good looking in a tight white linen manteau and elaborate makeup. Her speech was a little slurred and she seemed under the influence. It was not possible to have much of a conversation with her. Her "husband," a smallish young man with unbrushed teeth, was alert and on his cell phone. It rang frequently and he spoke into it confidentially and with cryptic formality. At some point during each conversation he walked away to continue out of our earshot. Occasionally I heard him giving directions and times. When he was with us he talked about doing good business and buying good things for his wife, although, he said, they still couldn't afford a house. She was principally interested in the dog and little boy.

At a little distance from us, a young mother in layers of black veil but with plucked eyebrows and discrete makeup shot disgusted glances at us. She officiously tended her toddler boy, repeatedly calling out his Shiite-overkill name of Amir Mahdi. Every time her son headed towards us she shooed him away. My son and Jennifer's owner were sprawled on the playground communing with the puppy. "Get away, Amir Mahdi. The dog is dirty. It will bite," the woman in black veil shrieked. A fashionably dressed young woman oblivious of soiling her white manteau, a young man making suspicious phone calls, an English-speaking boy with a lax mother, and an excited puppy were just the combination to evoke her disapproval. Her glances soon turned to squints.

Another night I encountered a group of young men

hanging out at the park. I talked to three of them while the fourth excused himself and played with my son the whole time. We had a long talk as the boys showed me different parts of the park. Two of them were in the first year of a "nonprofit" technical school and one was still in high school. One had voted for Mo'in, the "liberal" candidate, in the first round of elections and for no one in the second; the other had not voted at all; and the third did not say. (Voting age is sixteen in Iran.) They were cousins, originally from Bam, displaced by the earthquake, in Tehran via other cities where they had relatives. The conversation ran to life for young people in different cities.

"Our worst encounter with the revolutionary guards was in Kerman," said the more talkative one. "Our party was crashed one night and all of us—boys and girls—were taken in." The boys were severely beaten. One of the boys was hit so hard with a baton that his knees swelled up within minutes. After the beating they were ordered to do a hundred crouch-leaps. "I begged them to let me do push-ups instead," said the boy with the bad knees. "But they made me do the crouches. My knees are still swollen." I asked about the girls' treatment. "Girls are tormented psychologically. They are insulted, called obscene names in front of their cousins and friends," the boy said. "So they have learned to shut their ears to insults. They turn into stone." (Many years ago a friend of mine said that she figured out what revolutionary Iran is all about: Sex and violence.)

"But guys have their ways of getting even too," said the other boy. "Tell her about Mammad FBI." Mammad FBI was a brilliant friend of theirs, nicknamed in honor of his obsession with the FBI. They told me he studies the FBI with passion and is an expert in designing small concealable weapons. "He still hasn't finished actually making one," they said. They were proud of their friend and quizzed me on his behalf: "Does the FBI really know everything? What kind of weapons do they use? Can an Iranian join the FBI?" I tried to divert the conversation to interesting American and international organizations doing more constructive work than the FBI. At my mention of civil society and international organizations an interested middle-aged man joined our group. The young men politely listened with slightly glazed-over eyes.

While I was in Tehran an Indian friend of mine was in Bangalore working on a film about the effect of the call centers on that city. I tried to imagine young Iranians as cheap out-sourced labor for foreign companies. I tried to imagine Jennifer's owners and the other young men I talked to as customer service "associates." (Mammad FBI as tech support?) I was most successful envisioning Amir Mahdi's mother as floor supervisor, taking the corporate bottom line to heart and relishing the officiousness with which she bullied the rest of them.

The state of civil society

Sometime in the 1990s "civil society"—*jame'e-ye madani*—entered popular and official parlance. Loosely connected to Khatami's "dialogue of civilizations," nongovernmental organizations popped up everywhere and NGO became a familiar word. Over two thousand registered NGOs were listed in a resource publication by the end of the decade. While religious charities and "G-NGOs"—governmental non-governmental organizations—comprised a great many of the listed organizations, many impressive grassroots efforts were also made. Having contacts in a number of old and new civic organizations in Iran, I helped start a nonprofit in the U.S. to mobilize international support for the terrific work that they did.

Some of the best Iranian organizations were reluctant to make contact with international organizations. Never sure of how the government might respond to this attempt, they weighed every move with utmost caution. On the political level, there was skepticism about the motives of international organizations and fear on the side of the Iranians that they might inadvertently be pulled into serving hidden political agendas. On the professional level, many Iranian NGOs felt that by collaborating with international organizations they would end up doing the work—for no or very little money—for which the international organizations would get the credit. They were quite aware that lucrative "development" careers are made at the expense of local NGOs.

Nevertheless, the desire to break through their international isolation was strong and many NGOs agreed to work with us. Our gingerly steps came to a stop after 9/11 when even lip-service support in America for any democratic activity in Iran vanished. We were quite surprised last winter, then, to receive calls from American organizations to whom we had applied for grants years ago. Suddenly there seemed to be new interest in contacting civil society organizations in Iran and offering assistance. By this time, however, new reservations were added to the old ones about working with Americans. The war in Iraq had made Iranians uneasy about U.S. plans in the region. There was renewed mistrust and skepticism with respect to American organizations. Certainly any contact with Americans, let alone acceptance of assistance from them, was dangerous.

"We are dangling by a hair," one experienced NGO activist told me. "One controversial move and we're gone."

"Weren't some of the so-called civil society organizations that were involved in the attempted coup against Hugo Chavez in Venezuela funded by Americans?" another asked.

We declined the offers of assistance from the American organizations without having the chance to consult all our NGO "partners." With little time in Iran, and weary of the push to co-opt civil society by both domestic and international ulterior motives, I only talked to people I personally knew, letting them know of the interest of American organizations. Mainly I wanted to ascertain that we were right to have declined assistance on their behalf.

The people I talked to listened with interest, some with amusement. With the profound uncertainty brought on by the elections, any lengthy discussion about the pros and cons of international contact seemed a waste of time. "We have learned to live in bunkers," one NGO friend said. "Now we have to add a layer or two of reinforcement to the bunkers and hope to survive." But I saw that they were not passively sitting in their bunkers.

The Bam earthquake had taught the NGO community good lessons in preparing for the next disaster. An ambitious new umbrella organization of national NGOs and corporate donors was formed to improve coordination in the event of another emergency. A small group giving education and support to mothers on child-bearing and child-rearing issues had grown into a large and busy organization, and they had just completed a series of public education pamphlets, funded by the office of President Khatami. A children's literature organization founded in the 1960s had expanded into publishing books for children with various disabilities. A private foundation providing small loans in the form of sewing and fruit-drying machines to women heads of household had grown steadily. A center for street children, an offshoot of a children's rights NGO, had expanded its work to give services to Afghan and Arab refugee children as well. And small groups—from bird watching and eco-tours to consciousness-raising about domestic violence and restoration of old musical instruments—were formed by the dozens, frequently developing into full-fledged organizations.

Sadly, no one thought that the idea of contact with non-Iranian organizations—civil society to civil society, as it were—was plausible at the time. The only collaborations with international organizations continue to be mainly between UN agencies and the Iranian government. A well-known educator working with the children's literature NGO recently turned down an offer by a European organization to honor her. "We can't risk what we've built—and we don't trust them," was essentially what she said.

A decade ago it had seemed possible to help support and promote civil society organizations in Iran. Now we found ourselves conveying their "Thanks, but no, thanks" message to offers of assistance.

Uncivil society

The government notwithstanding, a major problem of building civic culture in Iran is the widespread absence of civility. People litter with complete ease as they call others *heyvan* (animal) for doing the same thing. Restaurant owners and staff ignore the patrons' unanimous complaint about deafeningly loud music once the food orders are made. Traffic regulations are for the birds.

It is the law, for instance, that motorcyclists wear helmets. So now riders zip through the traffic with helmets dangling from their handlebars, as if the object of owning a helmet is to avoid getting a ticket rather than surviving a crash. People seem remarkably unaware of both personal and collective benefits of civic agreements. No amount of motorcyclists sprawled in pools of blood on the street—not an uncommon sight at all—is going to get them to change their minds.

On a deeper level of tragedy, the looting that took place at Bam after the earthquake was particularly ugly. Some of it happened while there were still people alive under the rubble calling for help. A relief worker told me that while earthquake survivors in tents nursed a photographer who had fallen ill, the last of their possessions were being looted in what remained of their houses. People are very concerned about what would happen in a large city like Tehran in the event of a similar catastrophe.

As I looked at the many buildings under construction in Tehran I could not help but notice that the building material looked awfully shoddy. The new bricks were already chipped and cracked. Steel reinforcements, when there, looked terribly flimsy. It is estimated that an earthquake in Tehran of the magnitude of the one in Bam will kill up to four million people.

When this shoddy state of construction affairs comes up in conversation, the first object of blame is the mullahs. "They have brought us to this," everyone immediately says. (It is surprising that the earthquake in Bam was not blamed on the mullahs, the way the flood in Tehran in the mid-1980s was.) In a basically lawless country, there is very little regulation to protect the public and the sensible regulations that do exist are seen merely as obstacles to be gotten around with bribes. Government officials consider it their natural right to accept bribes from developers and contractors or the average bloke with a yen to improve his house. Neither side has any regard for the purpose of building codes. People's lives and the most basic principles of social contract mean absolutely nothing. These people are not mullahs; they are not necessarily Rafsanjani cronies; they are regular folk who, in their turn, do not hesitate to blame everything on the mullahs.

As I wondered what a civic response to this lack of regard for social contract could be, an interesting case of it occurred. A relative of mine owns a small unit in a well-made pre-revolution building. A few months ago, the small lower units were bought by a woman who clearly had no plans to live there. She started to remodel them in order to sell at great profit. She knocked down some walls, removed columns that supported the building, and even dug into the foundation. Soon, as the building shifted, cracks started spreading on walls in other units. City Hall officials put in an appearance early on but were silenced by her bribe.

The building residents were of course troubled. They formed an association to fight this new woman but felt they had little recourse. They knew that even if they were successful in the courts the best result would be a fine. She would swallow the fine of a couple million tomans and sell the renovated unit for close to a hundred million. The building would not be fixed.

By the time I left Iran, the residents' association was still debating what approach to take. Some argued that it would probably be less trouble to wait and see who buys the new unit. Their hope was that someone who wanted to live there would buy the apartment and in the interest of his own safety would consent to remedy the damage to the foundation and columns. The other tenants, of course, would have to share the expense.

A slow night at Mehrabad Airport

My friend Roya's American husband was arriving early one morning. I went to the airport with her at 2:00 a.m. to keep her company and be of help if there were complications. It was a slow night and we were early, so we sat outside on a bench to wait. A group of taxi drivers waiting for passengers were chatting among themselves. In a little while passengers from a plane that had landed from Jeddah cleared customs and trickled out.

"Asghar," called a driver to another who had just pulled in, "come give this *haj agha* a ride back to Jeddah." The *haj agha* (technically a man who has gone to Mecca, but liberally applied in Iran) was a tall man with a formidable belly in a long white djellaba. He was followed at demure distance by half a dozen black cones whose heavy veils with barely a slit at the eyes identified them as female. Their relative ease of movement hinted at their age. As the great patriarch strutted about, a couple of teenage boys in jeans and t-shirts—sons and brothers of the black cones, presumably—handled the family luggage. (Tradition? Jeans and t-shirts aren't exactly the traditional garb of the Arabian Peninsula.)

The Iranian cabbies snickered at the sight. "I wonder why they come here," one said.

"Well, for them Tehran is Paris," said another.

In contrast to the passengers from Jeddah, Iranian women and men at the airport walked shoulder to shoulder. While women were veiled in various degrees of habit and reluctance, their body language spoke of a sense of entitlement to walking beside men. Nor did I see an Iranian man strutting about paces ahead of his females.

The night before, we had gone to a concert by an Iranian woman singer. To perform in public is a right Iranian women have had to fight for after the revolution, but it is still against the law for a woman to sing solo—she must be accompanied by a man. One of the percussionists in this singer's ensemble accompanied her while she sang. He was a pro at keeping his voice almost inaudible in the background. I was impressed with the courage of the woman artist and touched by the self-effacement of the man artist. The absurdity of misogyny is so apparent in Iran.

At the airport, once the amusing diversion of the passengers from Jeddah came to an end, the taxi drivers resumed their conversation.

"It has gone up to fifty-nine dollars a barrel," said one.

"No, the latest is sixty-two."

"I wonder what they're going to do with the surplus."

"I just heard on the news that Iran has committed a billion dollars to rebuilding Iraq."

"Rebuild Iraq...? They still owe us damages for the war."

"If the American bosses say we rebuild Iraq, we rebuild Iraq."

"These gentlemen have to swallow it if they want to keep their power."

Then they fell silent—partly because the airport is not a safe place to discuss politics openly, and partly because the topic was just too depressing. They started watching the passengers again, discussing the foreigners.

A small group of European men, technical experts by the looks of them, walked out of the terminal. They acted upbeat and polite but made eye contact only with each other. They avoided the locals altogether and were particularly careful not to show any awareness of the female population. (There was no telling what those crazy Muslim men might do to them if they looked at their women folk.) Roya and I couldn't help staring at the Europeans with big smiles on our faces, watching them squirm under our gaze and making them feel as uncomfortable as possible.

"The Koreans," one of the taxi drivers was saying, "they're not really foreigners. They know all the exact cab fares."

The American's visit

My friend Roya and I had timed our trips to be in Iran at the same time. We live in different states in the U.S. and wanted to use the trip to spend time together and give our sons the chance to become friends. Roya had been in the process of obtaining a visitor's visa for her American husband for months. After filing an immense load of paper work with the Interest Section of the Islamic Republic of Iran in the Washington D.C. Pakistani embassy, she was told that policy had changed and the only authority that could now issue visas to Americans was the Foreign Ministry in Tehran. A first-degree relative had to apply in person at the ministry. The visa for Roya's young son—who as offspring of an Iranian woman married to a non-Iranian is not eligible for Iranian citizenship, hence the visa requirement—was issued in Washington. (Children of Iranian men married to non-Iranian women *are* eligible for citizenship.)

While the American husband waited in Istanbul, Roya applied for his visa in person in Tehran. I accompanied her on a couple of her many visits to the Foreign Ministry. In all fairness, getting a visa for an American to visit Iran was much more transparent and less humiliating—and costly—than getting a visa for an Iranian to visit the U.S. (This is noteworthy, since it is the president of United States who makes threats against Iran and not vice versa.) Roya's frequent visits to the Foreign Ministry warmed the officials to her and expedited things. Calls from family members in Istanbul to the Iranian Consulate helped with last minute logistics. It is still sometimes possible to humanize bureaucratic processes in the Iranian system.

On one of Roya's visits to the ministry her son and I were with her. She took the little boy with her from office to office and his presence charmed the officials. Not being overburdened with work, they chatted with him and looked at the books he had brought along. After leaving the office of one high-ranking official, the little boy turned to his mother, who despite her calm demeanor was still nervous, with a cocky five-year-old look: "You're a scaredy-cat, aren't you?"

He was not there to see his mother the day she had a face-off with one of the security guards at the door. When she was told that she could not enter because her pants were not of a solid dark color, she blew up.

"What is the point of this?" she said, raising her voice so everyone could hear. Everyone did stop, looking over their shoulders at the commotion at the door. "If you gave me freedom tomorrow I still would not dress all that differently from this." She was wearing loose pants with a button-down shirt over it. With "freedom" she would only have eliminated the minimal scarf on her head.

I watched the guard listen to her ravings with a hint of a smile. "Don't upset yourself," he said as he called on the phone the person with whom she had an appointment. "No, she hasn't brought her son today," he answered into the telephone at some point. She ended up having her business conducted even though she was not allowed inside.

When the American husband finally arrived, he did not encounter hostility except for some posturing at the airport. In fact, he was rather ignored. In the courtyard of the old Shah—now Khomeini—Mosque in the great bazaar of Tehran, as the mid-day *azan* filled the air, Roya's courage wavered for a moment and she told an enquiring bystander that her husband was Canadian. Immediately afterwards she felt like a coward—the "scaredy-cat" her son had accused her of. To the next person who asked, she boldly replied: "American."

One enquiring shopkeeper, it turned out, only meant the

question as a way of opening a conversation with our group. "So where do *you* live?" he turned to me after Roya.

I told him I lived in Tehran. "No you don't," he laughed. "I can see you're from Tehran, but you don't live here." How could he tell, I wondered. "Because you don't look *esteressed*," he said—"stressed," that is. At any rate, his real object was to divert our attention from a competitor. He threw a disparaging glance at the other shopkeeper whose wares we were eyeing. "Don't buy from him," he said. "The jerk voted for Ahmadinejad." Like all good businessmen he mixed politics and marketing.

I spent a good deal of time with Roya and her husband in Tehran. The American's response to the chaos of Tehran and the social and cultural complexities of Iran were more remarkable than anybody's response to him as an American. Only twice in his ten-day visit did he encounter any kind of reaction.

At the Sa'd Abad Palace compound that now houses museums, a member of the Revolutionary Guards asked for a light for his cigarette as we walked by. The American gave him the light and truthfully answered the question of where he was from. The guard grimaced. We could not make out hostility in the grimace—perhaps only an indication that what he had to say about America and Americans had to remain unsaid.

The second reaction was at the passport investigation booth at the airport when the family was leaving the country. As they arrived at the booth, one heavily veiled inspector, with military stripes on the sleeves that poked out from under her chador, traded posts with another. As the American passports of Roya's husband and son exchanged hands, the two inspectors made an inside joke and tittered. Neither had probably had much experience processing American passports, which held up the line to the irritation of other waiting passengers.

Roya's sociable little boy broke the ice with his timely "Salam" to the frowning inspector. With an unexpected smile in return she waved the American father and son through the gate to take seats while the Iranian mother stood at the booth.

Roya answered questions about what her husband did and the purpose of his visit, watched his name being copied on various documents, and they were cleared.

Modified terror

Let's say that, over the years, the reign of terror in Iran has been modified. The main target of harassment in daily life is now young people. This made my trip much more pleasant than in previous years. Gone were the days when my friends and I would be stopped and dragged to the *komiteh* for riding in a car with members of the opposite sex. Now I sailed through checkpoints no matter whom I rode with. The gray in the hair and the offspring in the backseat are now license for relative freedom. (Time to party, as a friend said.)

Apart from the personal convenience of being spared this kind of harassment I was glad of a finer point. Right after the revolution, gun-toting teenagers were unleashed on the population at large. At the time a young cousin of mine made the perceptive observation that giving young people the license to insult and mistreat people older than themselves is culturally out of place.

"It is not in our culture to be disrespectful to our elders," he said. "Are these guys not Iranian?"

Now it seems that a bit of the old regard for age has returned. And the presence of children does somewhat mitigate attacks.

But the war between rebellious youngsters and the morality police still gets bloody. The official term for these young people is *obash*—translatable as "riff raff" but with more insult packed in. One of the times we sailed through a checkpoint we noticed a car full of young men that had been pulled over for investigation. Armed basijis of about the same age were holding containers, full of booze we presumed, in the faces of the other boys. We, of course, discreetly moved on, but our hearts fell in our shoes thinking of what was in store for the young men. Late at night, you see inebriated boys tearing down the highways standing up behind their friends on motorcycles, screaming their lungs out. The religious hysteria of the basij evokes frighteningly self-destructive hysteria in the rest of the youth.

But I also witnessed cool and collected response to provocative Islamic hysteria. At the airport I was waiting in the long and tight line of passengers going through the "sisters'" security. "Sisters" refers both to women in general and the hyper-Islamic women guards who nowadays search handbags. Back in the old days, the sisters at the airport were daunting obstacles. You prayed that you landed a "brother" to search your suitcase. But there was no avoiding the sisters when it came time to be body-searched and have the contents of your carry-on combed. Now, the sisters' job at the airport has been modified. Now they are merely required to check your ticket and look at you with hostility as you go through the metal detector.

While I was waiting for my turn, two flustered young women cut through the line, excusing themselves profusely. It turned out that the sister who had checked their ticket made a mistake and told them that they had missed their plane. The young women had gone back to the airline counter to realize that the sister had read the date of their flight last night from Shiraz to Tehran instead of their present flight. So they were back and in a hurry to get on their plane.

"You gave us a shock," one of the young women said good-naturedly to the sister.

"You *need* to be shocked," the sister hissed in return.

The young women were determined not to be perturbed.

"You *must* be shocked," the sister repeated provocatively. "People like you need to be shocked, going back and forth between countries like..." she started to say *"ab-e emaleh"* (water from an enema) but she stopped herself. The Islamic Republic prides itself on its *effat-e kalam* (purity of speech).

The young women let the insult pass over their heads, adamantly maintaining their polite and cheerful demeanor. They cleared security and ran to their plane.

One day at the kindergarten where I sent my son, I noticed a Christmas tree in the corner. It was one of those permanent ones that you put up and take down each year, and it was hung with children's arts and crafts. I asked the principal about it: "Christmas tree in July...?!"

She said that for years she had been putting up a tree for Christmas in honor of her Christian students and also because it's such a cheerful sight. A couple of years ago she was visited by authorities from the Guidance Ministry and ordered to take it down. She told them that the tree was just decoration and had no other significance. "We keep it up all year long just to hang children's artwork," she said, thinking fast on her feet. After that, the Christmas tree had never come down.

Religious minorities have kept an awfully low profile in Iran since the revolution. Although there has been murderous treatment of Baha'is and menacing harassment of Jews, religious minorities, including Armenians and Assyrians (the main groups of Christian-Iranians) and Zoroastrians, have cautiously continued their lives. There is a silent requirement that they keep to themselves and stay out of politics. A friend told me that a Zoroastrian group that has been trying to register as an NGO for years is about to give it up. They are not denied outright, but they are subjected to a battle of attrition.

One day an Armenian taxi driver picked us up at the kindergarten. I said something in English to my son and the driver asked if we lived in the U.S. He said that he has cousins there whom he wants to join but his family is against it. He was quite distressed.

"My family says we must stay together in our country... but this is not my country," he said. "I hate this country. I hate the people. I hate everything about it."

Thinking about the relatively recent Christmas tree harassment at the kindergarten, I asked him if things had gotten worse since the revolution.

"No, it has always been like this," he said. "The bastards barge in on church services and insult the priests. They even interrupt funerals."

I was actually surprised to hear that. Islam, after all, does not separate itself from Judaism and Christianity (hence the bogusness of the notion of "dialogue of civilizations," especially on the part of the Iranians). Khomeini himself had called for letting adherents of other "religions of the book" live in peace. (Zoroastrians, even though they are not technically "of the book," are also included by virtue of being the original Iranians—though not the Baha'is.)

"*What* Islam? *What* God? *What* religion?" the driver nearly screamed when I said that harassing religious minorities is not Islamic.

What Islam, what God, what religion, indeed… There is a curious new development: Clandestine but well-organized groups of new converts to Christianity are popping up in Tehran. Evangelical TV programs broadcast from the U.S. provide guidance. Iranian converts in the U.S. help produce the shows, but there are apparently satellites in many places. The clan certainly has missionary zeal. I was propositioned in Istanbul by a very clean-cut young Iranian man who heard me speak Persian. He wanted to take me to see a new church and hear an interesting service.

I felt sorry for the Islamic Republic. Its flock seems to be fleeing in every direction.

The logic of cab fares

One day I rode with a taxi driver of especially dignified bearing. He was about sixty years old, well spoken, with intelligent eyes. I never did find out what he did before or besides driving a taxi. On our long drive from Toupkhaneh to Farmaniyeh in stop-and-go traffic, it was I who did all the talking. I leaned my elbows on the seats in front and vented in his ear. He listened patiently.

I ranted about how bad things are—about the Islamic Republic, the U.S., war, poverty, the chaos of Tehran. I expressed my disgust at the last election, the whole lot of the presidential candidates, and the fact that elections themselves have become such fraud.

Back when Khatami was elected for the first time in 1997, a window of opportunity for bringing meaning to "public participation" was cracked open. Khatami himself took some gingerly steps toward bringing the regime a step closer to toleration—not just toleration of lipstick and nail polish but toleration of people getting engaged in repairing this wrecked country and damaged society of ours. But that moment of opportunity had come and gone. It received no substantial support either inside or outside Iran.

I told the driver about the mother of a friend of mine who was arrested a couple of years ago with a group of young women for *bad-hejabi,* not being properly veiled. At the police station they all signed papers to the effect that they had acted in violation of article such and such of the constitution and in case of a repeat offence they would be subject to punishments according to article such and such of the constitution. Then they were let go.

This woman, wife of a prominent surgeon, did not let it rest at that. The next day she dragged her husband ("They don't take you seriously without your husband") to the police station, introduced him as the owner of one of the city's largest hospitals, and demanded to speak to the supervisor of last night's officer. Then, from her position of seniority of age and superiority of social rank, she proceeded to lecture him. She told him that this kind of harassment only creates hostility toward law enforcement and breeds anger towards the regime. Essentially, however, she conveyed that enough is enough.

The officer tore up the piece of paper she had signed the night before to assure her of a clear record. But she was not satisfied. "That is not what I came here for," she said. "I came back to personally ask you what message you think you are giving to young people with this piece of paper?" The officer said that the purpose of the contract was to educate young people that the country has a constitution and that its laws must be abided. It was, in effect, a lesson in democracy. (The U.S. spreads democracy through occupation and war and the Islamic Republic teaches it through harassment and jail.)

"Where do you even begin to explain what is wrong with this picture," I said to the driver.

At the heart of it is the question of the constitution. An Iranian public law expert told me that as long as Iran has the constitution that it does, democracy as it is commonly known is categorically out of the question. "What these guys have done is very clever," he said. "They have constitutionalized dictatorship."

Enshrined in the constitution of the Islamic Republic is the principle of *velayat-e faqih*, the guardianship of the religious jurisprudent—that is, the guardianship of the interpreter of Islamic law. This principle gives tremendous subjective power to clerics in interpreting religious law (a double whammy) and overrides any other article in keeping with the "good" of the country.

"Short of writing a new constitution—which means another

revolution—the only possibility for democratic reform is to ignore the constitution," the public law scholar said. "Maybe that's what Khatami quietly intended to do: adopt a 'don't ask, don't tell' approach to the constitution." But when the ideas of freedom and democracy become associated with ignoring the constitution, what hope is left for establishing the rule of law?

"There is a lot of talk about the religious law component of the velayat-e faqih," I continued with the driver. "But I have as much problem with the guardianship part. In both religious and civil law it is minors who are in need of guardians. Why is it presupposed that Iranian society needs guardians—are we a country of minors?"

The sad fact is that so much of the population does act like minors—incapable of taking responsibility or identifying collective interests. No wonder there are self-appointed "guardians" to determine what is "good" for them. How much longer are we going to blame littering, traffic, shoddy construction, corruption, and every other ill of the society on the constitution and its "guardians"? And what will wake up so many young people, the limits of whose imagination is the shedding of idiotic restrictions?

It is terribly disappointing that fashion, makeup, and nose jobs are the main expressions of dissent. It is alarming that the index of freedom should be joining the consumerism and vulgarity of the west that is destroying the planet and negating the most sublime accomplishments of the human species. In the early years of the revolution hundreds of thousands of young people perished in the war fronts and the prisons. While their youthful heroism was tragic and too often wrongheaded, there was no question as to their motives. They were driven by some idealistic vision. What kind of future are the young people now envisioning—anything that will amount to something substantially better than providing cheap labor for foreign companies?

At one point the taxi driver told me that people like me, who in spite of not living in Iran still concern themselves so much with it, remind him of children who will not abandon a parent suffering from terminal illness. I told him that to me it does not feel like the illness is outside of my body. "We all have the disease," I said. "And no matter how many times we are told there is no hope, that we don't have a chance, we won't give up the fight."

We are living organisms and, as such, we can't help but to put up a fight for life. Nonetheless, the prognosis is very, very poor.

The driver shot me a glance of sympathy in the rear view mirror. When we arrived at my apartment, he refused to take money from me.

"Az hozuretoun estefadeh kardam," he said. "I benefited from your presence."

I dedicate this book to him.

Returning to Iran

1986–1987

The joke is on us

From now on Iranians must plan their lives according to four givens: Khomeini will not die, the war will not end, Saddam will not go, Mahdi will not come.

I heard this joke in the summer of 1987. What struck me about it was its reference to the faint dawning of a reconciliation between the secular and the religious. For to the extent that the secular Iranian is likely to consider one leader immortal, another immune to fall, or even the most terrible war permanent, the devout Shiite is willing to entertain doubts about the coming of Mahdi, the twelfth Imam and Messiah. What the joke suggested was that through a circuitous route the most opposing rationalities could very well have arrived at a single conclusion. It is out of a shared sense of uncertainty and despair that such unlikely harmony appears to have emerged, and going back for the first time after the revolution I found naïve revolutionary solidarity beginning to be replaced by this more ironic reconciliation.

Yet the unspeakable reality of Iran still looms above taking consolation in any tenuous harmony. I spent the summers of 1986 and 1987 mostly in Tehran, taking notes almost reflexively, if only to be sustained through the horror of what I saw by the cathartic satisfaction of scratching the pages of my note pad with the sharp tip of my pen. The search for what is left behind by revolution, terror, and war became secondary to momentary escapes into note-taking.

Taking notes is a familiar escape for me. Boarding the plane in New York I automatically resort to my little techniques of avoiding eye contact with the passengers next to me. I adopted this attitude after the hostage crisis to avoid the dreaded question: Where are you from? When my answer does not evoke blatant hostility, it is received with a polite pause and the expectant look that I proceed to explain where I stand in relation to what has taken place in Iran, and, of course, the Great Satan. Try presenting the history of a country like Iran in a nutshell while taking care not to step on patriotic American toes or breathe on brittle American self-regard. It is draining. So I have come to try to avoid the encounter as much as possible.

On the plane I busy myself with writing in my notebook. For amusement I jot down some of the questions that I am usually asked. "Don't they hate you because you live in the U.S.?" is on top of the list. I note that an accurate response is only possible through an explanation of the dynamics of power, which has little to do with likes and dislikes. By the subtle choices in my particular variation of *hejab,* the "veil," for instance, "they" can determine in one glance my ideology, social class, and even subculture: "student," *ancien régime,* unreligious, or what not. They recognize me and I recognize them—but it is I who lays down her arms. "I am your enemy," my choice of hejab might suggest to them, "but you are in power," my demure presence in "their" airport acknowledges. I defer and they accept my deference. I dally in petty variations, but they determine the theme. And, yes, "they" may very well hate me for living in the U.S.—and this for a number of conflicting reasons—but travel restrictions are loosened at the moment and here I am.

But soon I have to abandon a certain tone and subject matter in my notes. There are countless lines and checkpoints to go through at Mehrabad Airport in Tehran. Not that it is feasible to go through every single passenger's personal notes upon arrival or departure, but should you be singled out for investigation for any reason, you naturally want to have minimized incriminating evidence against yourself. I remind myself to write only "personal" or "intellectual" things. I envision generating an article on Iran out of these notes and the semi-coded jargon that I develop.

I write that I must be a little out of my mind to be going on this trip. It is year eight of the Islamic Republic and my family is finally for the most part out. I have a dissertation that I could be writing, and twelve years after arriving in the U.S. as a foreign student, leaving New York City could very well feel like leaving home. What compels me, I wonder. I write of a certain restless discord that can eat at the insides of your life to leave it a hollow mound, or throw you at an exasperating pace in multiple directions at once. It can make you feel hollow and dense at the same time. Keeping up with the convulsions of culture and history in fierce interaction is not an intellectual challenge, it is a survival mechanism. And perhaps one has a lost a little hope as one has all too frequently watched one's western counterparts stop following one's words past a certain point. The straining of the common language you have come to rely on signals the beginning of a new alienation. Failing thus at communication, it becomes distressing to suspect that perhaps your English has gotten worse over the years.

This new alienation evokes different sensations than those early days of feeling foreign. There is something calculated about this, something inorganic. I think about American media. That the popular media thrive on objects of fear and hatred of Other origin is not new. The Russians and the Japanese have shared the stage with darker-hued peoples. Vilifying and ridiculing Germans is practically politically correct. That one "race," nation, or religion should replace another as enemy, or be added to a preexisting list in the popular imagination, surely cannot be more troubling because one happens to belong to it. The whole phenomenon is surely not intellectually unsettling. Or, at least, I cling to the hope that the images generated by the machinery of mass media will ultimately prove too fickle to withstand any real scrutiny. I wonder if evoking this sense of alienation is precisely the goal of a certain calculated effort and that I am succumbing to it.

To be fair, I go on to myself, I wonder if someone like me, really, is merely seeking to exhaust herself before succumbing to the charms of the west which happens just now to hold "exile" in somewhat of an intellectual fashion. And could you possibly, those discrete charms notwithstanding, blame your friends in the west for not having been pushed to the limits that you have been...? This is why I once again resolve, this time over the Atlantic, that it is indeed timely for people like me to examine the space, however tentative, they are occupying now. And it so happens that, seven years after the revolution, a number of my friends have independently decided to go to home.

The flight to Tehran is long and I stop my scribbling. And frankly, "identity"—and especially its resurrection in identity politics and, God save us, cultural relativism—is a tiresome preoccupation. So I am a nobody from no-man's land, a hybrid, a confused mess—big wow, what else is new.

Stepping off the plane into the dry heat of a summer afternoon at Mehrabad, embraced by the vital everyday Persian that I have not heard in a long time, the feeling is unmistakably that of home. An hour or two later, waiting in line to declare my foreign currency, I look over my shoulder at the *komiteh* booth that has just cleared me. The "brother" revolutionary guard who slapped my passport in front of me—the idea of touching whose hand I publicly declared repugnant, Islamic-fashion, by pausing a split second before picking up my passport with the tips of my fingers—is busily browsing his security roster. With an inward smile I recite to myself a line from Hafez, *Man as diyar-e habibam na az balad-e gharib*—I am from the land of the loved one, not from foreign parts—and have no doubt that my dark-bearded, brown-uniformed brother is also aware of this somewhere behind his knotted, Islamic fashion, brow.

And in the end, I think, who knows, perhaps all parties will be satisfied: Khomeini will die, the war will end, Saddam will be toppled, and even Mahdi will return.

Modernized and westernized

Iranians can't live without jokes. The tenor of the humor probably reflects national mood better than anything else. Even those of us who missed out on the early years of the revolution did not miss out on the jokes. By now, however, a new generation of jokes are making their appearance. Gone are the days of laughing off mullahs as bumbling ignoramuses. The chuckles over the dissertations of various ayatollahs filled with elaborate bathroom procedures and absurd pornography have died down. Hardly any trace is left of the gleeful celebration of revolutionary chaos. Now the jokes are darker and more ironic–and bitter.

In Tehran it is said that the main difference between the Iranian revolution and the French revolution is that in France the lumpen made the revolution and the intellectuals led it, while in Iran the intellectuals made the revolution and the lumpen lead.

Having your life and liberty in the hands of street thugs is certainly a bitter pill to swallow, but the bitterness does not end there. Living in the U.S., for example, it is hard not to be embittered by the apparently benign objectivity with which the title of "Islamic" is attached to the 1979 revolution. The "Islamic Revolution" is the catchword outcome of a rare (and ill-boding) collaboration between the news media and American academia.

Back in 1789 there was no talk of the "modernized" intellectuals versus the "traditional" *sans-culottes* ("populace," "proletariat," how ever way you look at it). It was presumed then, as it is presumed now, that all French people were French and citizenship was a universal right. But in the case of Iran, western "experts" point to the *cultural* failure of the Iranian intelligentsia, which by virtue of its more or less secular tradition and its exposure to the west is presumed necessarily "western," falling short of being truly Iranian. The long-standing participation of students, writers, artists, technocrats, and other segments of the population uncharacteristic of the "traditional" masses in the events that led to the 1979 revolution as well as the street confrontations that came to represent it notwithstanding, we are to humbly accept that it is not the usual complicated play of politics that has put the Hezbollah in its position of power, but rather its indisputable cultural authenticity. In a surprisingly anti-historical vein it has become the vogue in American academia to set the revolution in Iran apart from other social revolutions in the world. This revolution is seen not as demand for progress but as a reaction against it.

Then again, the very definition of progress is skewed when applied to Iran. In our case, "progress" is measured in terms of those amenities of modern life that are offered by technology, and by those aspects of western civilization that are primarily transmitted through its facilitation. It is defined in terms of adherence to western popular culture (in its most vulgar form, usually) and the embrace of what that culture (for lack of a better word) holds valuable. The "modernization" of Iran is then portrayed as the country's adoption of this kind of "progress." The verdict then is quick to follow that "the Shah modernized too fast." And we, the modernized Iranians, are seen as cultural mutants, byproducts of some newfangled policies of the Shah and his father.

One suspects that quite beyond the control of the Shah of Shahs, Modern Man ought to be credited with the creation of Modernized Man—after his own image, as creation goes. The result is that we, the "modernized" ones, have lost an identity as Other, gained one as Image, and been dismissed as ambivalent reflections of The Real Thing—oriental or occidental. This is not unique to Iran. Third-world intelligentsia are routinely brushed aside by their peers in the west. Our western counterparts think of us as watered-down images of themselves. They are not really interested in us; they want to hear from the "real" people. In Africa, "real" people are helpless and malnourished; in the Middle East, they are fundamentalist and violent mobs who know nothing about the west but hate it nonetheless. In the case of Iran, there is an inherent contradiction in the western practice of decrying the unknowable otherness of Islamic extremism on the one hand and claiming to see things from its perspective, on the other. It makes no sense for the modern ("western") world, bypassing its most logical link (us?) with what it sees as persistently pre-modern ("non-western"), to assume that it can go directly to the heart of Islamic fundamentalism and perceive us as aliens in our own culture.

But who exactly are we—the "modernized" ones?

Ideologically, a great deal of modern Iranian intelligentsia can be loosely defined as descendants of the *azadikhahi* movement that in its quest for freedom and democracy brought about the 1905 Constitutional Revolution. This was a movement in which a wide spectrum of the population participated, from bazaars and mosques to western-educated intellectuals, from progressive aristocracy to labor guilds. It was united within itself and with its more contemporary manifestation in the demand for national sovereignty, equity, and something to the effect of democracy. It was the enduring legacy of this movement, a vague and ill-defined idealism—as vague and ill-defined as any genuine and uncorrupted idealism by nature is—that never looked kindly on the Pahlavi dynasty. This was undoubtedly at work when on several critical occasions the Shah looked to the country's increasingly prosperous middle class for support but found little.

Culturally, I would trace my own lineage to the decidedly "westernized" intelligentsia of Iran—that segment of the modernized Iranians most acquainted with the west and most severely cast off by the Islamic Republic. We are the ones who, tarred and feathered, are paraded as "cultural failure" not just through the annals of Iranian-history-according-to-the-Islamic-Republic, but through the revered halls of American academe. As far as the latter is concerned, I wonder if owing to our multilingual education, we have shed our veneer of "otherness" and thus are seen as less capable of representing our, afterall, living culture now than when we were "exotic"?

Our political defeat in Iran is quietly being studied and many accounts of it are penned and stored underground until the time comes for their surfacing. As for our relations to the west, however, I will go so far as to say that the Islamic Republic is not alone in issuing *fatwas* against what it perceives as cultural transgression. If the Islamic Republic brutally silences Iranian intelligentsia inside the country, "expert" opinion silences it more subtly outside.

But as luck would have it, and silenced though we may be, we are not yet exterminated—neither inside nor outside Iran. We go about the business of writing our history quietly and perhaps in camouflage. We would be foolhardy at this point to insist on revolutionary strategies; the idea of a new beginning is sadly untenable. Considerations of feasibility and human cost inhibit the urge to start from scratch. In our relation to the west, insofar as we have inherited a "text," a history and an "ethnography" that it has authored upon us, it would be ineffectual for us to resort, as it were, to book-burning. It is, rather, by fully deciphering western testimonials of all types that we can hope to generate a common language in which to write. It has virtually become a methodological necessity to adhere to a decidedly old-school hierarchy of authority. We can expect to begin with the ingestion of a good deal of commentary, and graduate from the stage of annotation and interpretation of existing texts before attempting authorship of new ones. We may be spotted thus engrossed in the long robes and shaved heads of disciples, lugging about the great books of the masters, both oriental and occidental. There is nothing modern or modernized about this.

What's more, modern or traditional, secular or religious, whatever the ideology, there is at least one fundamental point on which all Iranian experience converges. I would venture that a signifanct characteristic of our national (un)consciousness is the conviction etched on our brains that things are not what they appear to be. Ours is a peculiar epistemology born of the dichotomy of *zaher* and *baten:* the appearance and the heart of the matter. Our historical experience confirms our philosophical predisposition only too well. The Iranian collective memory is drenched in the bitter realization that our best efforts are likely to work to our detriment—the recent revolution has certainly refreshed this memory. This bitter truth is especially affirmed by the high price that has been paid by participants in the entire spectrum of political action in Iran: from the price paid by those executed, imprisoned or exiled, to that paid by those martyred or disabled in the war with Iraq—a sacrifice that was ultimately washed down with a dose of metaphoric poison when Khomeini likened his ending of the war to imbibing poison. The Shah, who was savaged by both friend and enemy, certainly learned this lesson the hard way; the least he is due is the acknowledgement that he did after all spare the country a blow-out bloodbath before succumbing to his downfall. Perhaps those in power now will live to learn their lesson.

"Fear those whom you have served." I recently came across this quote attributed to Ali, the first Shiite Imam. Ali was not one for jokes but he too sounded bitter.

Women

When the Islamic Republic descended upon the heads of Iranian women like a massive, wretched beast, friend and foe in the west rallied to the rescue. From Italy, Oriana Fallaci trumpeted her call to arms.

In September of 1979 she interviewed Ayatollah Khomeini in Qom, the holy seat of Shiite Iran. It was a rare and symbolic audience: the emerging leader of Islamic Patriarchy versus Modern Man qua Emancipated Woman (donning a veil in professional accommodation). Excerpts from the interview were published in the New York Times Sunday Magazine in the U.S. and versions of it were reprinted in two Iranian newspapers.

Fallaci was well known in Iran from her books even before her famous interview with the Shah. The interview, in which the Shah embarrassed himself (among other things by declaring that women are inferior to men because even the best cooks in the world are men despite all the opportunity women have had in the field) had delighted the Shah's enemies and was banned in Iran. It was perhaps with a gleeful nod to that disastrous interview with the Shah that Khomeini agreed to sit with Fallaci. But readers, especially those familiar with Fallaci's confrontational style, expected a clash between the two at any moment.

The interview begins in earnest when Khomeini discloses valuable insights. He offers some key definitions, such as for freedom and democracy. As proof of the existence of "freedom" in Iran he gives the example of the masses of people who spontaneously poured into the streets at the death of

Ayatollah Taleghani. "Democracy" he defines in terms of a Shiite *hadith* (a narrative exposition of the Traditions of Islam). According to this hadith, Imam Ali and a Jew went to a judge to settle a dispute. The judge rose from his seat in Ali's honor but not for the Jew. Ali angrily denounced the judge for this discrimination and afterwards humbly accepted the sentence which was not in his favor. "Is there any better example of democracy?" Khomeini asks. He further explains that the notion of Islam contains the notion of democracy—which, incidentally, is why he rejected one of the proposed names for the new republic, the *Democratic* Islamic Republic of Iran. "Islamic Republic of Iran," Khomeini famously uttered. "Not a word more, not a word less."

Fallaci then brings up the emergence of what she calls "fascist fanaticism," that is, the violation of human rights on religious and political grounds such as the execution of Kurds and "counterrevolutionaries" and the flogging of women for improper veiling. This allegation Khomeini flatly rejects. Fascism is a western phenomenon, he explains; it just simply does not exist in Islamic culture. To avoid more discussion of this absolute, a priori notion, however, Khomeini resorts to one of the antics with which Iranians had already become familiar: he is struck with the fatigue that his advanced age entitles him to. But Fallaci doesn't back off—she brings up the question of women. She wants to know why women have to be deprived of their rights by the same revolution they helped make. Khomeini says that "elegant" women who show off their "necks and hair and shapes" did nothing for the revolution—nor anything good ever for that matter. "No, not those..." says Khomeini. "Those" only distract and upset men and fellow women.

It is too bad that Fallaci does not engage Khomeini in elaborating on his notions of the female body, that singular combination of beauty and evil that turns each woman into a most powerful she-devil. It is especially unfortunate that Abolhasan Banisadr, the first president of Iran, who was present at the interview, did not get a chance to expound his scientific theories on the existence of radiations emanating from women's hair that wreak havoc in the electrical integrity of the male system. Instead, Fallaci makes an attempt at poking fun by asking Khomeini how it is possible to swim in a veil. "None of your business," the Ayatollah replies; and to reciprocate the affront he adds that, anyway, Islamic dress is only for "good and proper young women."

Crash of cymbals, clash of civilizations: The confrontation that the reader was expecting arrives. Fallaci's buttons are finally pushed. She snatches the "stupid, medieval rag" off her head and flings it away: "There, done..." The suggestion that she is not a "good and proper" young woman is more than Fallaci can put up with.

Next, Islamic Patriarchy springs from his cushion on the floor ("like a young cat" Fallaci later described) and ends the interview—only to resume it the next day with no reference to the previous day's outburst. But Khomeini's tolerance of Fallaci's little act of rebellion is not entirely odd. It shows an inadvertent respect for a woman whom he admiringly describes as having widely traveled and "seen all forms of government," a woman who "knows history." (Any other Iranian praising a woman in these words would be called westernized.) Fallaci, for her part, is also a bit smitten with the "Imam." (If I were religious I would swear to God that before the revolution the reverent use of this title was reserved only for the twelve Shiite Imams, all direct descendents of the Prophet.) She later said that meeting Khomeini was the first time she encountered real charisma.

But—clash or mutual admiration of civilizations aside—what about Iranian women?

Throwing temper tantrums over the medieval rag is not an option for Iranian women. They have learned to swallow their modern rage and perceive the *hejab* as the political phenomenon that it is—and to trivialize the thing in itself. In fact, one could say that the most pervasive and systematic act of resistance against the Islamic Republic has been the untiring experimentation of Iranian women with maintaining autonomy, dignity, and, indeed, feminine beauty in the face of the humiliations of the hejab.

The veil, or more accurately, the women's uniform of the Islamic Republic, has become an ever-renewed vehicle for expressing pride and dissent paired with the most frivolous statements of fashion. (To be sure, men have their loosely defined and less strictly enforced uniform too: Nehru collared long-sleeve shirts worn untucked over loose pants, preferably accompanied by various lengths of untrimmed facial hair.) For women, the latter-day hejab, the *rupoush* and *rusari*—the long, loose overgarment and the head scarf—are acceptable in place of the old-fashioned *chador*. In keeping up with the times, shoulder pads appear underneath the rupoush. Perms become popular to combat the limpness that results from covering hair day in and day out with clinging head scarves. Lace gloves make a comeback to begrudgingly cover painted and manicured fingernails.

One particularly elegant woman with an acute postmodern sensibility has a series of overgarments made for her with the cut of the *'aba* (the mantle of the mullahs) which she wears over matching "Kurdish" pants. Shunning the astronomically priced ready-to-wear European imports that are marketed around the new Meydan-e Mohseni (where many a wife of a mullah is spotted shopping), she has her patent leather *na'leyn* (backless slippers, also part of the mullah attire) custom-made for her at the old shoemakers' row on Bagh-e Sepahsalar street.

Quite significantly, those Iranian women who did not grow up wearing the veil have developed the same keen kinesthetic sense that their *chadori* sisters master early on. This is the sense that allows a woman a good degree of control over the "accidental" slipping of her chador or rusari. A stray lock of hair makes its strategic appearance and disappearance; the bare neck most unintentionally emerges from under its coverings to happen to catch the light (and hopefully a breeze); the glint of a gold earring flashes in and out of sight for the split second it takes to attract attention.

A dancer I know found a welcome sense of freedom in

being released from the constraints of structured western clothing. She moved about in her loosest, longest rupoush, gloating in the new facility with which she had learned to "project" from underneath the drape of soft fabric. "Think Isadora Duncan, think Martha Graham," she said. But her friends' snide remark was that she got the idea from Peter O'Toole in Lawrence of Arabia.

Nevertheless there is little to be done about the knot of the rusari that presses like the tip of a dull knife at the throat. This is a constant reminder of the price that is paid daily for the vengeance with which women fight the demonization of the female body. I talked with a sixteen-year-old who was picked up on the street on account of *badhejabi*—being "ill-veiled," that is, below or in aesthetic violation of official standards. She was given the option of 30 lashes or a 30,000 toman fine. (Over the years, as the economy has worsened, cash fines are offered as alternate to flogging.) She chose the lashes. After a whole day's detention she and her fellow detainees were given permission to call home. She refused the call because, she said, if her parents had learned of her situation they would have scraped up the money and rushed to bail her out.

"But I would rather let them worry a bit longer and go home without having made a cash contribution to the Islamic Republic," she told me. "Besides, you can't expect others to pay a price for the choices you make."

In contrast to the anything-but-confused fight of Iranian women against the hejab, the western enthusiasts of this struggle are often blinded by the righteousness of their adoptive cause. If the hejab covers the bodies of Iranian women, it certainly seems to veil the otherwise sharp faculties of their western friends.

A good demonstration of this occurs in the Fallaci interview. After the interruption over the medieval rag, Fallaci continues with questions on cultural and religious differences. Khomeini summarizes his perspective on East/West relations: Western science and technology are acceptable but western "ideas and customs" are not. At this point it is pretty clear that neither side likes the "ideas and customs" of the other—that's fair enough. But had Fallaci not been derailed by her own righteous indignation—or maybe if she had been a bit more clever—she could have foregone sensationalist declarations of cultural difference to take note in this very interview of subtle leads into the darker corners of the Islamic world.

For instance, on the topic of Islamic polygamy (the Koranic right of Muslim men to take up to four wives) Khomeini gives Fallaci the classic defense that more women are born than men and more men are killed in war than women. Now, given that the number of female births relative to male cannot ever have been double, let alone fourfold, if there is any validity to the equation it must be due to the number of men decreasing in war. This explanation suggests that just as it is the Islamic *custom* for a man to marry more than one woman it is also the *custom* to regularly pack off large numbers of men to be killed in war.

In Tehran people note that the morality brigade of the Islamic Republic, the Monkerat (the fleet of Revolutionary Guards and their heavily veiled female counterparts known as the Sisters of Zeynab who enforce the Shiite decrees of *amr be ma'rouf* and *nahy az monkar*), takes to the streets for flogging and fining bad-hejab women just when there is a particularly bloody confrontation at the fronts. Apart from creating distraction, the practice tries to drive home the point of a ubiquitous slogan, a "message" from the Unknown Soldier/Martyr: *Sister, your hejab is more devastating for the enemy than the shedding of my blood.* It is as if the flogging of an inadequately covered woman somehow makes up for or reinforces the effectiveness of a man's death.

A curious connection between the subjugation of women and the shedding of young men's blood nags at the mind. To me it suggests that if a legacy of Islamic patriarchy is the oppression of its daughters, it is also the murder of its sons. On the wall of a rehabilitation center for disabled veterans (the "living martyrs") on Iranshahr Avenue, across the street from *Behdari-ye Sepah* (a large hospital for the Revolutionary Guard

Corps), a most gruesome verbal expression of this connection is presented by a slogan attributed to none other than martyr par excellence, Hossein, the fourth Imam: *The death of one's child is more beautiful than a necklace on the neck of a young and beautiful girl.*

I copy the phrase in my notebook hoping to fathom someday the connection between female beauty and the death of young men. I am particularly baffled by the message this slogan, at this particular location, delivers to the hundreds of thousands of physically and psychologically mutilated veterans who seem to have deprived someone somewhere of the beauty of their death by remaining alive.

Yet of course Islam did not invent patriarchy and its myths and institutions, and the quotation above, one hopes, in the worst event of proving verifiable, must have been uttered by Hossein the Innocent under very unusual circumstances.

To bring the matter closer to home, one has only to recall the ancient Iranian epic, the Shahnameh, which is a long narrative of sons begotten and raised in pride only to be murdered by their fathers in rivalry. Rostam, the arch hero, avenging the blood of Siavash for which his father the king of Iran is responsible, and agonizing over the trap set for Esfandiyar by his father, another king, has the blood of his own son Sohrab on his hands—a murder caused as much by wounded vanity as treachery and misunderstanding.

King and Hero are joined in this common destiny, and the mourning of Tahmineh, Farangis, and Katayoun, mothers and wives, runs like a subterranean river through the text of the great tragedies. Over time, with the intermingling of Iranian and Islamic rituals and traditions, the tragedy of the family of Ali—that single most enduring outlet for the expression of Shiite passion—is drawn into this great Iranian capacity for mourning. *Siyavashoun* and *Ta'zieh,* passion plays keeping myth and history alive in the memories of Siavash and Hossein, grieve the shedding of innocent blood. This ancient grief is bitterer to swallow than modern rage.

Tulips and poppies

Behesht-e Zahra (Paradise of Zahra) is the name of a huge cemetery outside Tehran on the highway to Qom. Conceived and partially built before the revolution, it is being rapidly filled, though not quite finished, as if testifying to the fulfillment of a grotesque prophecy. There are areas designated for common folk dead of common causes, for martyrs of the revolution (those killed on the streets in 1978-79), martyrs of war, and even executed political prisoners.

Entering the grounds very early on a summer morning, having left home at dawn to avoid the mad traffic of downtown Tehran and the scorching midday desert sun, we are relieved by a gentle breeze drifting from a generous stream of fresh water running through the main boulevard. A row of fountains spouts into the hot air enormous volumes of precious water that is piped across vast arid plains that produce little more than a few basketfuls of scrawny eggplants sold by barefoot children on the side of the road.

Visiting the cemetery is considered virtuous in Iran. It is customary for large family groups to spend whole days at the gravesite of a departed relative. Women are left alone to wail or pull their veils over their faces and silently weep. Men, laying a hand lightly on a tombstone, may recite a *fateheh,* or drift off quietly talking among themselves, while children run about and play. Trees and shrubbery are therefore essential for people to take refuge in the shade—to eat their lunch or take naps.

The area of Behesht-e Zahra containing the common dead is developing into an oasis. Lots here are planted with greenery and flowers with greater or lesser degrees of care. In some parts, luscious flowering plants bloom in defiance of the unrelenting sun, while in others overgrown weeds and nondescript wild plants cover neglected tombs. Water faucets are plentifully provided and visitors fetch water to rinse the dust from their relatives' gravestones. The dead and the living alike partake of the cool water that is almost miraculous in its ubiquity in the heart of the desert.

At the epicenter of the area designated to the martyrs is the now famous Fountain of Blood. This is a multi-layered, circular cement construction with a single fountain in the center of the smallest uppermost level. The fountain oozes a red liquid that falls in thin ripples from each level to the one below. The liquid is watery, not quite as deeply red as blood, and the structure is most disturbing when the fountain is turned off; the cement platforms bring to mind the permanently stained floor of a slaughterhouse. It is difficult to assess the site's impact by the expressions of the passersby. Faces show nothing.

The fountain of blood is a symbol without an agreed-upon referent. It was erected as a tribute to the legacy and legitimacy of martyrdom, but it represents more readily the human cost of the legacy of the Islamic Republic. Mourners and visitors stay clear of it for the most part now that its unsightly novelty has worn off. Children avoid it in favor of the water faucets on the periphery of the fountain area, where they hover over the gushing water and wash their hands and faces tens of times over.

To drive the point home, however, the Islamic Republic brings the fountain of blood to families individually. I have heard that a miniature replica of the fountain is sent to stand by the door of the house of a recent martyr—but they seem to quickly disappear. Traditional *hejlehs,* on the other hand, are visible everywhere throughout the cities. These chandelier-like structures lit by gas-burning lamps symbolize the wedding chamber *(hejleh)* of a departed unmarried youth. Standing on street corners and decorated with glass and crystal tulip-shaped candleholders, they display a flower-strewn framed photograph of the dead young man. At night, the light trapped in the cuts of crystal gives off a melancholy glow around which the friends of the deceased gather in their black shirts. The hejleh stands for forty days and nights.

At Behesht-e Zahra hejlehs are brought to mind by the glass encasements raised on metal stakes on the graves of many martyrs. These are the families' private contributions to the otherwise officially laid-out landscape of the *Qat'e-ye Shohada* (Martyrs' Lot). They may contain combinations of childhood photographs, a poem or two, letters or other memorabilia, a copy of the Koran, plastic flowers. The permanence of these simplified forms of hejleh call for artificial flowers, since the contents of the sealed-off glass shrines are not easily accessible.

While hejlehs are posthumous celebrations of male virginity, tulips are symbols of martyrdom. A red tulip is the flower par excellence that springs from the earth where innocent blood is shed. The Islamic Republic adopted this symbol early on and displays it pervasively. It is printed on stamps and posters commemorating the revolution. In crude sculptures it stands in front of government buildings and in town squares. It is donated in one form or another to families of martyrs, and, of course, it "springs up" in any cemetery.

Entering a small town in Gilan, travelers are greeted by a floating banner that declares: "The tree of Islam grows on blood." The town square is encircled by a metal fence in the shape of entwined long-stemmed tulips on which are posted photographs of the young men of the town whose blood was offered to the tree of Islam. In the Martyrs' Lot of the local cemetery, overgrown with the semitropical greenery of Gilan, the huge, brightly painted red tulip memorials erected on individual graves give off a hollow metallic ring when awe-stricken and dazed children bump into them.

Deeply ingrained in Persian poetic consciousness, the most conventional representation of this symbol is literary. The *laleh* is as likely to appear in canonical texts as in folklore, and most recently it has come to permeate the lyric utterances of revolutionary fervor. The title of a short-lived collection of poetry which appeared soon after the revolution and was printed several times, "Tulips of Shahrivar," is an allusion to the massacre of "Black Friday"—Friday the 17th of Shahrivar, 1357 (September 8, 1978)—when troops opened fire into the crowd demonstrating at Jaleh Square. "Tulips rising from the blood of the country's youth" is a favorite cliché phrase of the Islamic Republic. And the metaphor is developed as in a poem titled "Behesht-e Zahra" in a monthly publication of the Revolutionary Guards Corps, *Payam-e Enqelab:* "For the blooming of a single tulip / The flower of joy withered in the gardener's heart. / The bed of tulips springing in this plain of sorrow / Must be called the stream of the Blood of God."

But in the burial ground of the political prisoners at Behesht-e Zahra, neither water nor flower is permitted. This lot lies on undeveloped outskirts of the cemetery. Driving on the wide, paved road surrounding the area—taking care not to slow down conspicuously—visitors can observe shattered tombstones, broken glass, and upturned earth. Bodies are buried here anonymously, and should the family of an executed prisoner find out the location of a grave and place a stone over it, the stone is promptly crushed by the authorities. Some families designate an approximate location by a secret landmark, while others who dare to visit the lot grieve over any and all of the undistinguished graves. Very infrequently a particularly brave family might leave flowers behind, introducing a temporary speck of color in the wasteland landscape.

Recently executed prisoners, however, may be buried in the areas allotted to the non-political dead. These graves, no longer anonymous, are dispersed among the new lots to minimize the possibility of a politically motivated congregation. By matching the inscribed burial date on the grave of a friend's executed husband we could find a few other such carefully tucked away graves. Prisoners are executed in planned-in-advance batches. But even not knowing a particular burial date an acute observer can pick out these graves: The stones are plain, bearing no words of lamentation or poetry, and the birth dates usually fall within the last two or three decades.

A friend whose husband was executed a couple of years ago told me that she felt lucky to have a place to visit. She takes the bus to the cemetery after work every Thursday evening, bringing flowers and pouring fresh water over the sun-baked stone of her husband's grave. She also goes to make sure that the stone on which, in defiance of the authorities, she had a red poppy engraved remains intact. Keeping an eye out for visitors of other execution graves, she often spends her evening in their company, camouflaged in the heavy traffic of weekend common visitors.

Khayyam is not a poet typically quoted on tombstones. In his *dahri* world view death is too material, too final, and too utterly devoid of tribute to individuality to be of consolation to most people at the death of a loved one. But I was surprised to come upon a single Khayyam line on a neglected stone somewhere on the margins of the lot dedicated to the martyrs of the revolution:

> *Beware not to reveal this secret:*
> *A withered tulip will not bloom again*

What you see and what you hear

*D*aneshgah-e Melli (National University) is built on the hills overlooking Evin valley. On a hot late morning, my friend, a former student of Melli University, and I walked up the hill to the entrance. We walked past the old university guard headquarters that was built under the Shah as a security measure against student demonstrations and political rallies. The once dreaded site is now home to families displaced by war. Little boys played soccer with a limp ball and took turns riding a rusty oversized bicycle. The neglected headquarters, lined with drying laundry, would perhaps have been a welcome sight to the protesting students before the revolution, but it remains bitterly ironic in the eyes of the terrorized and veiled new generation of students.

We were turned away at the main entrance to the University on account of our hejab not meeting official standards (the color not dark enough), so we entered through an out-of-the-way gate that my friend remembered. The sturdy and once immaculate buildings of the campus (this used to be, after all, a fashionable university) through seven years of turmoil and disrepair have turned into mock echoes of the quest for knowledge. The slogans on the walls silently mirror the noisy rhetoric of the Islamic Republic. *We have no need for non-Islamic institutions*—Imam Khomeini. *Our revolution is a revolution of values*—Imam Khomeini. *The pledge of our academics must be to Islam*—Imam Khomeini.

We walked to the gym and straight on to the southwest porch where we looked down on the wide expanse of Evin prison. A massive brick wall covered with electrified barbed wire and punctuated by observation towers continues in and out of sight along the rolling hills, engulfing square miles of desolate space.

The vantage points from which the prison compound is so panoramically displayed used to be guarded and kept off-limits by the university guards before the revolution—a situation that provoked the students even more and drove them to despise and abuse the perfectly groomed soccer field and the shining sports equipment that filled the various halls of the gym. But the Islamic Republic does not insist on keeping secrets. The Imam, addressing his Cabinet during the Week of Government in the summer of 1986, declared, "It does not matter if our economy is bankrupt. The important thing is that Islam is not bankrupt." It is in the same no-secrets spirit that the Republic exposes people to the graveyard of its executed victims and students to the sight of its prisons and even to the sound of its firing squads.

The panorama of Evin serves a function for Melli University beyond what the site of the *Namaz-e Jom'eh* (Friday Prayer) serves for Tehran University. Shortly after the revolution, the soccer field at Tehran University was paved over and turned into the stage for the Friday Prayer. The area is wire-fenced in and faces a painted blue, green, and yellow pulpit—a vague landscape of a sky and a sun—which displays a large photograph of Khomeini and smaller ones of the "martyred" Ayatollah Beheshti and Khomeini's heir-apparent Ayatollah Montazeri. Before the midday prayer, a semi-automatic-toting preacher high in the power hierarchy—the President, the Speaker of the Parliament, the Prosecutor General, or the like—delivers a sermon or two that sets the tone for the social and political atmosphere of the following week.

Modeled after the early Islamic display of Muslim unity and power, the Namaz-e Jom'eh in Tehran is a resurrected ritual that in the age of mass media has increasingly turned into a spectacle. Each Friday dawn the streets surrounding the university area are closed off to traffic as thousands of men, women, and children—the *ommat* (*umma* in Arabic) "folk," of

Hezbollah—are bused in and arranged in sections and rows designated by special markings that are regularly repainted on the streets.

The televised image of the ommat in prostration, then on their feet on cue, stringing together a series of "Death to..." slogans, and shaking clenched fists into the camera, often finds its way into many a faraway living room. By late afternoon, buses transporting the last groups of women, drenched with sweat underneath their heavy veilings and carrying heat-struck small children, vacate the area leaving the neighborhood to enjoy a brief respite, after hours of blasting speeches and screeching microphones and before the return of the noise and fumes of resumed car traffic. On weekdays, the special markings on the streets—signifiers of the farcical and violence-infused Namaz-e Jom'eh—blend with unheeded traffic signals into an even larger gridlock of ignored signs.

The impact of Evin, on the other hand, is that of a referent. The panorama of Evin is not meant to symbolize, and while accessible to a live audience, the still-life vista is not meant for video cameras.

Two main buildings comprise the compound of Evin Prison. A red brick building that operated under the Shah was "liberated" Bastille-style in 1979 with the intention, people now recall almost with amusement at their own naiveté, of turning it into a museum. Next to it stands a yellowing cement construction about three times larger whose foundation was laid before the revolution and was speedily completed by the Islamic Republic.

The interior layout of these buildings is impossible to reconstruct from descriptions. Visitors and prisoners both are blindfolded as they are taken inside or moved about in the buildings. Prisoners who are allowed to visit with their families—for ten minutes every forty-five days across Plexiglas and through telephones—are led to the visiting room in a row, blindfolded, holding each other's hands, a rope, or the corners of each other's veils. Visitors are screened at an office located in an amusement park (Luna Park) across the highway from the main prison area, where in the evenings children are treated to their meager, wartime ration of recreation.

One woman who spent four years in Evin said that she had begun to get a feeling for the architecture of the place: the *bands* (communal units) each consisting of one room, one hallway, one communal washroom, and the guards' quarters; the infirmary; the yard; the solitary cells; and the approximate distance and relationship of these spaces to one another.

Another woman who was released after only one year had a much vaguer notion of the layout of the buildings. To assess her direction she studied the light coming through a barred window high up on the wall in the hallway. At one point, she found shadows of leaves playing on the wall and floor, by which she concluded that the building must have multiple levels. But before she could map it out more clearly, and as other prisoners also discovered the little display of the outside world and spent time hovering over the play of light and shadow, one day they found the window draped with a piece of cloth.

Another day, the four-year-old son of a prisoner (living with his mother in the all-woman *band*) climbed on the shoulders of one of the women to take a peek at the sky through a bent ventilation shutter in the shower stall. He reported seeing a man, lying behind a door, singing to himself. The child reported "blood" and "chains." Encouraged by the women, the little boy greeted the man, calling him "uncle," and held a cheerful conversation until it became too risky to carry on.

Adara is the Arabic root for the verb "to be absolved from guilt." *Ta'zir* (in the Persian pronunciation), meaning "to absolve from guilt," is the word used for the act of torture by the prison system of the Islamic Republic. Amnesty International defines torture as "isolation, humiliation, psychological pressure and physical pain [as] means to obtain information, to break down the prisoner and to intimidate those close to him or her." The word *ta'zir* does not deny any of this; it only carries with it the divine justification that in the process, the prisoner is absolved from any guilt—that of which he or she is accused or suspected by the Islamic Republic, or any other. The former Revolutionary Prosecutor General Ayatollah Khalkhali once proclaimed, "If these people are guilty they are hereby absolved, and if they are innocent they become martyrs and will go to heaven." Savak, before the revolution, denied torture but at least called it by its name.

I talked to a number of people who had experienced Evin. When I spoke to M she had been out of jail for less than a year. At the age of sixteen (year two of the Islamic Republic) she was arrested for distributing leftist leaflets. She spent the next four years in Evin and Qezel-Hesar. Soft-spoken and iron-willed, she had survived experiences details of which she spared her family. During our conversation she ate her lunch, drank her tea, peeled fruit for her little cousin, and went on and on about what she called "the other facts of life." Her mother watched us anxiously from the corner of her eyes, torn between wanting and not wanting to hear.

M had not been cooperative with prison authorities. She had disobeyed many rules: She had given curt answers during her interrogation; she had comforted and emboldened other prisoners; and, most importantly, she had never volunteered information, significant or insignificant. For her unyielding behavior at Evin, she was first punished by a stretch of time in solitary confinement, and then was transferred to the even more sinister Qezel-Hesar prison. She said that she found solitary confinement more tolerable than the communal *bands*. She had bent a smuggled safety pin into a hook, pulled threads from her blanket, and crocheted. She learned to communicate with other prisoners by a coded banging on the walls. But, mostly, being left alone with her thoughts was what she found least objectionable. After her transfer to Qezel-Hesar, where it was forbidden to hold a conversation or share food with others in the *band,* where inmates were forced to sit for hours in the morning and hours in the afternoon in front of repeated propaganda videos, her health began to decline. At Evin she would stand motionless under the ice-cold showers in the winter as frequently and for as long as she was allowed—it gave her strength, she said—but at Qezel-Hesar she was beginning to lose, as she put it, "the energy to be human."

During her time at Qezel-Hesar, the head of the prison was a man by the name of Haj Davoud (referred to simply as Haji) who has since been dismissed, allegedly on account of his unusually cruel ways but possibly because of factional differences. The pride of his establishment was the infamous Unit One, nicknamed *Tabout* (The Coffin), which was a large room divided by waist-high wood planks into a number of "coffins." Prisoners were confined to these structures, blindfolded with their hands tied behind their backs, sitting upright without back support and with their legs stretched in front of them—sometimes for months at a time.

The idea was to devise a method for prolonged torture that minimized the chance of death and loss of urgently sought information and which did not leave physical scars. The silence of the room was periodically broken by a fit of crying or a prisoner standing up in her coffin, who would then be taken away to "write." She would be given a supply of paper and left alone to put down the entire content of her memory, relevant and irrelevant to her accusations, until she was emptied.

Haji was known for bringing in bouquets of flowers every now and then and declaring: "I am holding fresh flowers from the garden outside. Would anyone like to smell the flowers?" He would even sometimes bring in his newborn son and ask: "Would anyone like to hold a baby...?" He would urge: "Come on girls, stand up, speak up, look what you're missing." And often the prisoners who did smell the flowers or touch the baby would "stand" and "write." M never experienced Unit One. Soon after her transfer to Qezel-Hesar her health began to deteriorate, her energy dwindle, and she broke no more rules. Unbeknownst to her she was serving the final months of her jail term. Within four months she was returned to Evin and then released.

On the campus of Melli University, we visited my friend's old department. One of the janitors recognized her and both their faces lit up as they talked about the old faculty members and students of the physics department. He told us that the majority of the professors in the department now only have Masters degrees and the PhD students resent having to work with them. He said that he did not blame the old professors, those who had not already been subjected to *paksazi* ("cleansing," purging, of establishments by dismissing socially and ideologically undesirable employees) for quitting. He said that my friend brought with her good memories and he was afraid that he would talk our heads off. He told us of the nightmare of finding milk or baby formula for his eight-month-old son, of standing in lines from four o'clock in the morning and at eleven being told that the supplies had run out.

"They say let your wife breastfeed," he said. "You will forgive me, it is rude, but my wife is not a cow. She doesn't eat *chelokabab* for lunch every day either. She is wasting away trying to fill the baby's stomach."

He asked if we had heard the rumor that recently a man driven to despair over finding milk and medicine for his infant had suddenly lost his mind and smashed the baby on the pavement in front of government representatives. (We had.) He told us that by his calculations—considering inflation, black-market prices, mandatory "contributions" to the war, and no raise in six years—his income was worth far less than half of what it had been before the revolution.

As we prepared to leave he grew increasingly heavyhearted.

"But I must say this," he said. "I feel forever indebted to the Imam. He has done us a great service." We were taken aback a little. He continued: "Because now I can be sure that my children and grandchildren will be rid of Islam once and for all."

On the run

Boys over the age of fourteen are prohibited from leaving the country. By the age of eighteen, those who have not already volunteered for *Basij* or joined the *Sepah-e Pasdaran* are drafted into the army. The Basij—dubbed *yek bar masraf,* the "disposables"—is a volunteer militia corps ranging in age from very young to quite old. It recruits among the poorest of the urban and rural populations and provides minimal military training before dispatching the volunteers to the fronts. Sepah-e Pasdaran (Revolutionary Guards Corps) is in command of the Basij. The Sepah, also a volunteer corps, is privileged with material comforts and a good deal of much-feared authority.

Young men who do not fall victim to the ideological and social pressures of Basij, who have something to lose, or who do not wish to claim any stake in the economic and power structure of the Islamic Republic are drafted into *Artesh*—the Armed Forces of Iran. These men are simply soldiers. In their khaki uniforms—injured, amputated, deranged, malnourished, lost—they may roam the streets of Tehran begging for food, "bus-ticket home," or some such. They may populate the unrecognizably overgrown city of Shiraz in search of opium, hashish, or heroin. Or, of course, they may return home from service and continue with their lives.

In Tehran I met a soldier from Dasht-e Moghan on the Soviet border in Azarbaijan. Strong and athletic, F had volunteered to join a special-forces unit after being drafted. The appeal of access to a gym and the "commando" image had quickly worn off, however, after he was sent to fight in the mountains of Kurdistan. This is an unpublicized front and, from the perspective of the Iranian soldier, a death-trap. Subjected to nearly constant Iraqi shelling, he is attacked by guerrillas from the Mojahedin and other opposition groups gone awry, and is pitched against Kurdish rebels with whom he sympathizes more often than not. He has a slight survival edge over a Pasdar who is murdered on the spot if captured.

F told me that Kurdish fighters check the cartridge of a captured soldier's weapon, and if he has not fired any shots his life is spared. Soldiers, therefore, take turns covering for each other when they are commanded to shoot in battle: on any given day there are those who shoot and those who only go through the motions. But even if a captured soldier's life is spared, he is expected to fight on the Kurdish side—this time pitched against soldiers like himself.

Due to the extraordinary danger of the area soldiers are required to serve only three months at this front. This particular soldier, unruly by nature, had deserted the army soon after being drafted. He had spent three months with sisters and brothers in various towns until he was persuaded that a voluntary return might be his least risky alternative. He had returned and requested a court martial with the hope that he might be judged untrustworthy for the sensitive paramilitary operations in Kurdistan and transferred to the southern front. Seven months after his return he had still not been court-martialed. Even after accumulating a record of brawls with his commanders and distributing "counterrevolutionary" poetry, F was kept on in service and a state of limbo. Since paramilitary operations translate primarily into survival tactics, a soldier with enough tenure to master these skills is too valuable to let go of.

When I met him, F had acquired a medical leave of absence by claiming "brain damage" (he had feigned fainting spells and bouts of "madness"). With the help of a lucky home-town connection he was sent to Tehran for brain scans. This had bought him fifteen days, but he knew that the results of the tests would surely send him back to Kurdistan.

He hoped that the escalation of confrontations in the Persian Gulf would temporarily lull activity on the Kurdish front and buy him more time.

In Istanbul, I talked with K, a young man who had dodged the draft by escaping Iran through the Pakistani border. There is much smuggling on the Turkish and Pakistani borders. Many Iranians, fearful of persecution or simply unable to cope, have paid large sums of money to be smuggled out of Iran. To leave the country illegally, of course, means giving up the option to return.

K recounted for me an anxious but smooth escape in diverse company: an older couple, a young woman with her son, and another young man running away from the war. Luckily there had been no nightmarish twists in the escape—no confrontations with Revolutionary Guards, no middle-of-the-way abandonment by smugglers, no struggles against inclement nature. K recalled a silent and beautiful sunrise across the border into Pakistan and great relief upon arrival in Karachi. The group met their smuggler in a hotel where they were given their documents, after which each was to go his or her own way. The last hurdle was to clear the authorities in Karachi airport—or else join the faceless crowd of Iranian refugees stranded in Pakistan.

At the hotel, physically and emotionally exhausted, K and his friend treated themselves to a long bath before sleeping. The next day they arrived at the airport the very models of upright conservatism, alert and clean shaven, dressed in their single change of clothes—the suits they had hung in the steamed-up bathroom the night before to smooth the wrinkles from being packed in the small carry-ons that they had been allowed to bring on the escape.

For their flight to Istanbul, they waited in line at the Turkish Airline counter behind a group of western youth in scraggly beards and permanently soiled jeans. Anxiously clutching their documents, the young Iranian men watched the bleary-eyed western youth present their authoritative passports, on whose magical wings they seemed to travel to any destination in pursuit of, mostly, byproducts of hemp and poppy. Our friends checked their bags and the large radio and cassette player one of them had bought in the Karachi black market.

One last time, the Turkish Airlines clerk asked for their papers, and looking them over, in the official interest of protecting his country from the onslaught of Iranian refugees, he announced, "Your passports and visas are forgeries. We cannot take you on." Unprepared for this last attack, the friends momentarily despaired. Driven to emergency measures they made a desperate personal plea. "You may be right or you may be wrong," one of them said, "but your decision carries a lot of weight."

The employee continued to stare at them from behind the counter. They implored again, "We are students and we need a chance."

Finally, after a pause that locked their breath, the airline employee handed them their boarding passes. Without once having looked around, their dazed western peers had already boarded the plane when a Pakistani police officer called K and his friend aside for a final, farewell strip search. The one who had not spent his money on a boom box lost it to the officer before they finally boarded.

Two years later in Turkey, pulling himself out of a deep depression, twenty-year-old K "baptized" himself—as he put it—in the Black Sea and faced his world head on: He studied composition at a music conservatory in Istanbul while his childhood friends fought in the war back home. This was his life, and the allowances of youthful crisis existed for none of them any more.

The martyr and his creator

Payam-e Shahid (Message of the Martyr) is an everyday tribunal for the rhetoric and politics of the Islamic Republic. A clever propaganda device, it reiterates stock sentiments and injunctions in a new context each time. Sometimes, when it is actually the words of individual men, it also provides a first and last chance for a great number of faceless sons of poverty to claim existence and, however prefabricated and short-lived, a voice. It is a tribunal for Man-as-Martyr-of-the-Islamic-Republic.

Payam-e Shahid appears in different forms and greater or lesser degrees of authenticity. Sometimes it is an anonymous signature validating a spray-painted slogan: *Sister, your black hejab is more devastating for the enemy than my red blood.*—Payam-e Shahid. Other times it may appear in an eclectic anthology of poetry, described as a scribbled sentence found in the pocket of a man killed in confrontation with the Shah's forces on the streets: "If I die, leave my eyes open so it will be known that I did not die in blind faith."

More elaborately and less anonymously, it appears regularly in weekly and monthly propaganda magazines published by various organs of the Sepah-e Pasdaran or Basij organizations. These are passages excerpted from farewell letters and "wills." In the magazine format, Payam-e Shahid appears as brief messages accompanied by photographs of martyrs (sometimes as children, sometimes as corpses), the date and place of their martyrdom, and code names of the offensives in which they were martyred. (The biographical information does not reveal their dates of birth.) These messages are for the most part statements of loyalty to Islam, Imam, and the war:

> "With the passing of each martyr, our responsibility becomes greater. We must mobilize our forces and proceed to the fronts."

> "Follow the Imam and do not refrain from joining our brothers at the fronts, lest our revolution be endangered."

> "Our revolution is the precursor of global Islamic Path. It must be exported to every corner of the world."

Longer messages are combinations of testimonial, apology, and simple personal letters. They are often addressed to a family member and speak of passion and longing that surpass earthly love. One addresses a mother:

> "I know that the sorrow of losing a child is great. If I ask you to forget me, mother, I would be demanding an impossible thing from you. But life is short and sooner or later we all must go. So much the better if death comes as martyrdom in the Path of God."

Another message salutes Mahdi and Imam Khomeini "from the bottom of a heart bereaved with a burning love":

> "Brothers and sisters, know that I have found my Path and I will follow it to the end. I have gone to fight the enemies of Islam, for Jihad is war and war is the illuminator of human essence. Jihad is the gateway to Heaven through which the martyr passes. I know that I do not deserve the honor of martyrdom, but if I am granted this honor, know that it has been my dearest wish. I am ready to be resurrected a hundred times and killed a hundred times in the Path of God."

"I prefer to speak my heart tonight. Maybe the purpose of writing these letters is to gain momentary respite from the heaviness of a certain burden. But, alas, the love in my heart is inexpressible. My son, I was destined to look after you only for a short while. Now that God has called me to Him and will be receiving me soon, I ask for your blessing. You, too, must make an offering, your father, to God:

"He who dreamed of the garden / Offers the seeds of martyrdom / To earth—heavy earth—so there may be hope for new blossoming / For the season is a sterile season."

But who is the martyr?

In a piece titled "Unaddressed Letter" in an issue of *E'tesam* magazine, a high-school teacher writes the profile of a martyred student. It opens: "The felling of martyrs is their rising, their bloodied sleep their awakening. They are trees that will never know autumn for they shed their leaves in the spring of their lives. They have chosen the season of their bloom for their departure, but their true life begins with their death..." He proceeds to recount his reservations in writing a biography of his student: "I fear that such a biography will only contain the vocabulary of pain, suffering, and poverty. What other words are there to be found in the glossary of life experiences in southern Tehran...? But these *divans* are also filled with long *qasidas* on faith and devotion. Let us call our martyr Reza, his father Pain, and his mother Deprivation."

"Reza" is in eighth grade when he volunteers for the Basij. "A life so short hardly warrants a 'beginning' and an 'end'," his teacher writes. "I taught him to pray. One evening after his prayer I saw that he would not rise from prostration. His thin shoulders were trembling and when he finally rose, his large eyes were brimming with tears. This time it was he who taught me about prayer."

Reza is killed and the author addresses him in a letter that, sadly, can never be sent: "Keeping my promise to you,

I went to see your mother. She had just returned from the burial and was smiling through her tears. 'I kissed him,' she said to me, 'I kissed his cold cheeks'."

Despite the ideologically noncommittal words of the mother the teacher approaches her: "I spoke only briefly with her. It did not seem necessary to speak much, for she seemed to know it all. We cried together. I wanted to say to her: 'Let us eliminate the word "death" from our language. In the vocabulary of martyrdom there is no such word'."

Deprivation as virtue is not a notion unique to Islam. To exemplify the Shiite variation, here is a *hadith* from Koleini from Abi Basir:

> "A blind man goes to Imam Baqer [the sixth Imam] and asks whether the Imam can perform miracles such as the Koran attributes to Jesus. The Imam touches the blind man on the eyes and his sight is restored to him. 'Now, would you prefer to remain a seeing man,' the Imam asks, 'and be judged on the Day of Judgment like the rest of men, or would you rather be blind and go to heaven without judgment?' The man chooses to revert to blindness."

By this logic the deprived, the meek, the innocent, and, naturally, the very young, precisely because they shall not be judged as harshly as others who are less virtuous, can be sent off to die more readily. By another logic, it is not their deprivation, their meekness, or even their youth that deems these men innocent. Their innocence is in their motivation for going to war: not to kill in hatred, but to die in love.

But where does the yearnings and dreams of adolescence end and the unrequitable love of God begin?

Oblivious to this lack of distinction, the propaganda magazines spell out for us that Love provides the force toward martyrdom, and that Purification of the Self is the preparation. Articles are regularly run on the virtues of purification and the means of achieving it. "Islamic Ethics: The Self-Making of Man" is the title of one such article. It advocates *'Aql* (Reason) as a controlling power over "internal forces" that lead men to selfish and ultimately criminal acts. 'Aql prevents men from seeking momentary gratification and guides them toward decisions of long-term benefit—that is, gains in the hereafter. Another article preaches Patience and Perseverance: "Patience in the face of difficulty and unfortunate accident is the first order of purification. Patience in delivery of obligation and duty is the second order. But patience in refraining from sin is the highest order of purity."

Often these articles prove forbidding for an outsider as much because of the method of their arguments as their ideological content. In "Guidance in the Koran: The Necessary Relationship between Man and Religion," for example, the argument runs something like this: "For every being a state of perfection exists which is distinct to it, and for every such state there is a singular path leading to it." "Law" ensures that the individual does not stray from the correct path: "Law is nothing other than pragmatic wisdom," while "ideology is wisdom in practice." Every ideology has its corresponding *jahan-bini (Weltanschaaung)* from which follows a "practical and religious wisdom that familiarizes man with God and the Day of Judgment." The argument concludes: "There is only one religion and one school that guarantees the theoretical and practical perfection of man."

Reading the article carefully I was left with the impression that law, religion, ideology, *Weltanschaaung*, wisdom, and so on, are all in some circular fashion connected to each other and to "Islam," and the whole of the muddy logic originates from one premise which is, one might say, man's Will to Perfection:

> "Question: Is it correct that the desire for perfection *[meyl be takamol]* exists in all beings?
> "Ayatollah Motahhari: This is a philosophical principle. Such a desire is an a priori condition of man."

Thus it appears that in what the teacher of the martyred student called the "vocabulary of martyrdom," we are given "love," "quest for purification," and "desire for perfection" to substitute for "pain, suffering, and poverty." But the stock phrases that are endlessly repeated in a sampling of Payam-e Shahid seem to strengthen the suspicion that the vocabulary of man-as-martyr is infinitely more limited than the vocabulary of the slums of Tehran, rich with humanity as they are.

Furthermore, purification of the self is a problematic issue. It is by definition a never-ending process, a circle out of which Practical Man must break to leave Religious Man behind. In an article titled "With what Motivation Must We Go to the Fronts?" the conflict, however, is surprisingly easily resolved. We read that it is imperative for "brothers" to know and purify their motivations before they enlist. (Which is perhaps, among other things, an involuntary confirmation of the appeal of cash compensations for the families of martyrs.) The article lays out guidelines for proper soul searching. The conclusion, however, is most sobering:

> "1. Those brothers among us who are on their way to the fronts must be of the conviction that their action is for the sake of God alone, and they must purify their hearts of any other intention and motivation.
>
> "2. If the brothers do not succeed in purifying their hearts to the desired degree, they must not use this excuse to neglect their duties of defending Islam and our Islamic country."

In other words, not even the quest for purification—the Will to Perfection—must interfere with the march towards death. Or as a Persian proverb says: *Ze har taraf ke shavad koshteh naf'e Eslam ast*—Death from either camp (friend or enemy, "pure" or otherwise) is to the benefit of Islam.

Finally, an editorial expounding *Tajdid-e 'Ahd- e Tarikhi* (the re-commitment to, the re-engagement with, history) locates the martyr in time and place:

> "The appearance of these selfless youth in our times

is indeed a wondrous miracle beyond comprehension of reason. A calculating mind might say that these youth merely swim against the current, and superficial eye may confirm this. But history unfolds in the hands of those who free themselves from the trends, habits, and expectations of the times. It is they who accept the mission of rescuing mankind from the grip of its attachments and subjugating devotions, of material necessities, dictates of society and nature, and other constraints. If all men abandon themselves to the flow of the dominant current, how shall the evolution of our history be realized...? These youth are qualitatively different from those ignorant and slothful others, mostly inhabiting our cities, who remain forever disconnected from the great stage where history is realized."

The time is present par excellence: the very moment of realization of history *(tahaqqoq-e tarikh)*. And the place is the battlefronts at hand: the "plains of sorrow," the fields of tulip where the Blood of God is let.

So it appears that this time around, for the realization of history, God is being murdered in Iran.

Repent, repent...

Taba is the Arabic root for "to repent." *Tavvab,* in the Persian pronunciation, is "the repentant one." In the vocabulary of the prisons of the Islamic Republic, tavvabs are those prisoners who repent their "counter-revolutionary" and "divisionist" pasts and see the light of God on pain of death. To the extent of their degree of cooperation, tavvabs enjoy privileges and authority within the prison system. They may be allowed to distribute food, ration the tea, or keep an eye on the activities of fellow prisoners. Tavvab women may be chosen by male guards as mates for *siqeh* (temporary marriage) and occasionally rewarded with frivolous contents of confiscated handbags.

I heard of one tavvab who had fallen in love with Lajevardi, head of Evin Prison, and shed tears of longing over a newspaper clipping with his photograph. Others might accompany Pasdars on their patrol rounds to identify former neighborhood associates for interrogation. Some with a good enough record might be allowed to visit their families at home for twenty-four or sometimes forty-eight hours. Often they inherit tasks that prison authorities reject.

One such task is tediously putting together disparate information extracted from prisoners. A tavvab may be given, for example, the most illegible accounts written by prisoners and required to reconstruct and diagram the hierarchy of a prisoner's contacts within a "subversive" organization. It is a task somewhat like assembling a triangular jigsaw puzzle, which when completed depicts one high-ranking member at the peak, followed by a few lesser ones, and branching out progressively to include all the prisoner's contacts.

The most rejected task, however, is not a bureaucratic one. This is the ritual finishing off of executed prisoners. With the firing squad watching, certain tavvabs are known to have demonstrated their utmost loyalty by firing the final shot into the head of a fallen man or woman—perhaps even a one-time comrade.

On the street one day after their release from Evin, Z and two of her former prison mates ran into a young woman tavvab whom they recognized in spite of her heavy veil. She ran away from them in horror. Z's friend, who was well informed in these matters, explained that released tavvabs have good reason to fear identification and revenge. The friends later learned that this particular woman had voluntarily returned to Evin as a guard and continued to live in the *band* where she was held prisoner. Tavvabs are broken people. "Repenting" a former existence, denying the past, does not leave a person whole.

The anthology of *Rouzha va Souzha* (Days and Scorchings) is published by the Ministry of Islamic Guidance, Division of Prison Supervision. Sometimes it contains essays—passionate but unreadable ideological critiques of one opposition group or another—but mostly it publishes poems and stories by repentant inmates from Evin and Qezel-Hesar. In the introduction to the first of these volumes we read:

> "The merit of this collection is that it uses art to convey the message of prisoners who used to belong to groups hostile to the revolution. This is a message born of a culture that, despite its long-standing existence, has unfortunately never been presented as such. Many of its aspects have been explored in other more direct forms, such as interviews or reports, but these can never deliver the message with the effectiveness of a work of art."

The "other" forms of expression referred to by the unnamed author of this introduction—televised (usually closed-circuit inside the prisons and sometimes on national TV) interviews and published "reports"—are familiar devices of propaganda warfare used by both Savak and the Islamic Republic. They are known to be quite ineffective in convincing the public of what the regime wants. Neither the eager nor the stony faces that appear on the television screen now and then, speaking of their misguided and criminal past, inspire conviction in viewers. But these are not meant to convince the public. They are used to break spirits.

The writer of this introduction quotes Tolstoy, "the great and religious Russian writer," as defining literary art in terms of the transference of an experienced feeling from writer to reader. The "sincerity of emotions" which, according to this article, characterizes art is the missing element in official interviews and reports:

> "Let others say what they may... Let there be talk of the use of drugs and force in extracting repentance. Once you have sat with these people and listened to their accounts of regret, suffering, and longing, you can judge for yourself the sincerity of their words. Art—exquisite and effective art—is like a hand opening a pomegranate, inside which you can discover for yourself the lusciousness or the decay of the fruit."

The anthology offers instances in which the "culture" mentioned in the introduction is actualized in writing. There persistently appears the sweet and peaceful moment of embracing death—death wish pure and simple:

> "Tonight my heart roams our city like a stranger. Silence cloaks the sleepy streets... Pure is the scent of the orange blossoms and sweet is the sorrow running in my veins. My heart travels the dark road to the graveyard of our city."

The moment of final surrender is drawn out and savored in a story about a railroad worker who sacrifices his life to save a passenger train from crashing into a collapsed tunnel. Told in second person narrative, the story ends with a passage describing the worker's body lying lifeless on the snow:

> "How slowly you take your final breaths... You are glad to leave the tracks of life behind and no longer be a captive to it. You would smile, but you no longer have the strength. In a few moments nothing will remain in your memory and you will know no one... You think of the high flight of eagles and your eyelids close in peace. The pleasure of this eternal sleep rests softly on your face."

But the culture of repentance must by definition also celebrate a new beginning. In a poem titled "A Narrative of Sleep and Awakening" we read of "awakening" through being consumed by fire:

> "Now that I burn in the fire that I myself have set / I speak of my sleep and awakening... / From the extremes of humiliation / I speak of eternal shame, / Of a strange but newly familiar sorrow."

In the anthology's short stories, this awakening, this new beginning, appears in different interpretations. In a lyrical story it may be the protagonist's discovery of the serenity of a certain mosque to which she used to be indifferent. In a zealous piece, it may be presented as a new commitment to the cause of Islamic justice. Often it takes the form of a transformation that takes place in a woman as a result of an act of self-sacrifice on the part of a man. The relationship between brother and sister is a recurring context in which attachment, conflict, and resolution are examined. Through this transformation process a sister's perception is altered in ways prescribed by the brother.

In "The Shattered Mirror" we read of the political "subversion" of a young woman who comes from a devout religious family, her alienation from them, and her reawakening following the martyrdom of a brother. The story opens with the news of the protagonist's acceptance to the university, immediately after the revolution when some degree of political activism still existed on campuses. Sadiqeh is seduced into a movement with a rhetoric of "toiling masses" and "comrades" and is persuaded by her new associates to exchange her customary black chador for the lighter *rupoush* and *rusari* worn by women of less pious backgrounds.

She wears the new garb whenever she is away from her own neighborhood, and she feels torn by her loyalty to an organization that calls men like her two brothers serving at various fronts "mercenaries" and runs contrary to the beliefs of her widowed mother. She is repeatedly warned by her old friend Masoumeh, who attends the same university (but in black veil) and witnesses Sadiqeh's change of personality, and by her mother who instinctively senses distance and danger. Without her veil Sadiqeh feels exposed and uncomfortable, and the pressure from her friend and mother is constant and unrelenting. At one point, after an unpleasant encounter between the two friends on campus, we read:

> "[Sadiqeh] was touched by the ease and lightness of Masoumeh's movements. For a moment she wished that she too would wrap herself in her veil and at once be free from all this confusion and anxiety..."

One of her brothers returns from the front having lost both legs, but Sadiqeh persists in her new ways. She even goes so far as to expand her contacts within the organization and finds herself working directly under a male associate. As her previous contact, a woman, introduces her to the new man, they all shake hands:

> "Sadiqeh stretched out her hand reluctantly. This was the first time she was shaking hands with a man. She felt his warmth and was overcome with feelings of shame and sin. She quickly withdrew her hand and was overwhelmed

by the sensation of her own descent into the fires of hell—
the heat of which seemed to emanate from the warm joining of their hands."

The moment of confrontation comes when Sadiqeh's second brother, Javad, runs into her on the street in her liberated costume. His rage is blind and fierce, and she half expects to be murdered. This happens two days before Javad's departure for the front. After receiving a good thrashing at his hands, out of fear and shame Sadiqeh locks herself overnight in the cellar. Persuaded by her mother and invalid brother to make peace with Javad before he goes off to war, she emerges from the cellar the next day. Javad is calm and understanding. She collapses into his arms:

> "She devoured the scent of his body and the rosewater sprinkled on his shirt. Tears flowed on both their faces and mixed on their cheeks. Sadiqeh liked the taste of his salty tears on her tongue. They remained motionless for a few moments. Javad moved his lips to his sister's ears and she felt the roughness of his whiskers on her skin. Sadiqeh felt that he had something important to say to her and she listened with her entire body. Javad whispered in her ears, quietly, only for her to hear, 'Sadiqeh, sister, you must never forget God... Just remember that other than God everything is a mirage and nothing more. I shall be leaving but you who remain must know that you cannot live without God.'"

When Javad's body is brought home in a casket, his mother and sister are calm. Looking at Sadiqeh's bewildered face, her mother says, "My innocent daughter, I understand that the sorrow of living without a brother is great." The family is glad that Sadiqeh had made peace with Javad before he was martyred. When Sadiqeh finally breaks down at his burial, she pulls back the white shroud in which his body is wrapped and sees that his skull is crushed and his eye sockets are empty.

She wails and the congregation wails with her. At home she tries to collect her thoughts in solitude.

Roaming absentmindedly in the yard, she walks to the pool and sorrowfully addresses the goldfish, "*Salam.* I've come to be reconciled with you. This is the Sadiqeh who loves you. This is Javad's Sadiqeh." When she dips her hands in the water she feels the fish slipping through her fingers. She recites, "*Astaghforellah-e rabbi va atoba elayh*—I beg God's forgiveness and I repent." Then she unfolds her long-untouched prayer carpet, dons a white veil, and goes down in prostration.

> "Then she saw Javad again. He was standing tall before her, smiling. She too rose, and muttered *Allah-o Akbar.*"

The author would of course have us be content with Sadiqeh's transformation, reverting back to her original self. But another reading is possible. Sadiqeh's commitment to the leftist movement is a transference of her family's devout faith to a new cause—a cause whose adoption is her way of rebelling. But as her rebelliousness is crushed, her passion is redirected homeward to what seems to be the very object of it: her brother. Sadiqeh's uninhibitedly sensuous love, such as she describes while in her brother's arms, must never find expression outside of the family.

In "On Leave for a Few Days," the relationship between sister and brother is presented in yet another aspect: the dependence of the sister on the brother, not only in the correctness of her perception of the world but in her ability to perceive at all. This is the story of a revolutionary guard, Said, who returns home from the war for a few days, his regrets for having survived his martyred friends, his benevolence toward their families as well as his own, and his assassination by "terrorists" on the street. The story is told by his sister, Maryam, who is hungry for his teachings. She recalls that before going off to the front he had a long talk with her: "I understood him perfectly, as if I had known it all before... Indeed a brother is his sister's eyes."

He had said, "Maryam, I hope that you will never become like Mojdeh and Nayyereh who have nothing on their minds but pretty clothes. Today I saw them on the street wearing gilded scarves on their heads. I wish they wouldn't do such things—the scarves shone in the sun like chandeliers... Sister, pray for me to be martyred. All my friends are gone. I have fallen behind. I am the only one left." Maryam had answered, "Don't say these things, brother. I don't want to lose you. If you die I will be blind." He had responded, "No, sister, the Imam is the eyes of us all. Pray that he lives forever."

After Said is gunned down on the street, Maryam takes to reading his books: "I have learned many things from him. I have learned how to learn." She speaks to him in her dreams and his image is always with her: "Now I don't have to wait for him to return from the front. I know that he is dressed in white, like an angel, floating in the sky above our house. Last night when I closed my eyes and my tears were trapped between my eyelids, I seemed to fly over the seas with him. A red tulip had grown on his head. I flew with him. I was no longer afraid—not even of horseback riding and swimming. He taught me everything."

She continues, "The terrorist who shot you was blind. He could not see how you left the earth like a green tree and ascended into the sky. Now he cannot see that like a white dove you are forever aloft." She decides that from then on she will no longer be "Maryam" but "Rafideh" who, a footnote informs us, was a "sister nurse who served in the tent of the prophet."

For a sister's ability to "see," even when her visions seem more like surrealistic hallucinations than Islamic Truth, a brother must give his life. For a correct or improved identity of a sister—Sadiqeh's return to her old identity, Maryam's transformation into Rafideh—the brother must be sacrificed. The blood of the brother is the salvation of the sister.

The color black

The entire country is pervaded with the color black.
This is not the solitary and sorrowful black we are accustomed to see worn in mourning for forty days or a year. Nor is it the dramatic black of the banners of the *Tasu'a* and *Ashura* mourning processions, flying against a backdrop of white cotton and green silk, bringing to life the massacre of the Seventy-Two Innocents and drawing tears from the great Lion of Persia. This is a new color.

It can be the color of lead, opaque and overbearing, as the painted-over windows of the white building of Hotel Chalous turned interrogation center and prison. The windows of the charming old hotel are slathered in black and people walk or drive by in feigned obliviousness lest they arouse the suspicion of the Pasdars lining the building's roof and porches.

Chalous and its neighboring Noshahr, small towns in Mazandaran province on the Caspian coast, were favored by the Shah and his father as summer resorts. Before the revolution these towns prospered from waves of summer tourists from Tehran. They became associated with decadence: nightclubs, luxurious private villas, and bare female skin on the beaches. Even though now the villas are for the most part abandoned by their exiled owners or confiscated by the various Islamic "foundations," and women are allowed to bathe only in carefully secluded and patrolled areas in pants, overgarments, and head scarves, these towns are still subjected to more than the usual degree of Islamic surveillance. On any hot and humid morning, a rusty Peykan of the Nowshahr police, with its makeshift new Allah emblem, patrols the streets warning the population through an ancient portable loudspeaker of the punitive consequences of badhejabi and other social offenses. An off-white Nissan Patrol of the Revolutionary Guards, with a Peykan-ful of Sisters in tow, silently circles the streets.

Or the black can be glossy and piercing, as in the glance of revolutionary guards following your movements when you walk by. It cuts through our animated conversation one day as I descend the stairs of an apartment building into the street with my friends. I am in the company of three men to whom I am unrelated—an offense punishable for all of us by flogging, at least—when we unexpectedly come face to face with a sight we must ignore and leave as quickly as we can. A man behind the steering wheel of his car, deathly pale, answers the questions of the Pasdars hovering over him. His car is cornered by three Nissan Patrols against which other guards lean, pointing their G-3 semi-automatics in our direction and following our steps with their eyes. We lower our voices, do not altogether stop, and walk briskly but casually to our car. One more time we escape being the immediate subject of their attention.

Black is the color of fear. J, picked up in a phone booth by virtue of being in the wrong place at the wrong time, or perhaps simply because of "suspicious appearance," is strapped to the *ta'zir* platform, and flogged for information at Sho'beh 5 of Evin. She is beaten on the bottoms of her feet with wire cables. Not particularly exotic, this most common form of ta'zir has proven to serve the purpose well. J is left alone when her feet become numb but the ta'zir session are resumed when the wounds have "cooled off"—which in Evin parlance means the feet and legs have swollen and the nerves have become active again. She is periodically left alone with pen and paper to write her confessions. She is confronted with other prisoners who might recognize her, or she them, before being transferred to a room where detainees—bleeding, delirious with pain, or temporarily insane—are kept between sessions of interrogation.

Strapped down, intermittently conscious, J lives the

timelessness of pain. She remembers nothing, she knows nothing, but pain. Sometimes she is left for minutes, sometimes for hours. Unable to anticipate the next ta'zir session, the boundaries of pain and fear of pain give way, and she succumbs to the permanence of the moment. She falls asleep when she is left alone to write. She falls asleep under the lashes, frustrating and provoking her interrogators even more. In the communal room she grabs hold of the skirt of a woman who stands up with a jolt in the middle of the night shaking her head and muttering, pulls her down to the floor, and they both sleep.

Blindfolded, you see nothing but black. Tied down on the ta'zir platform with your head covered by a folded blanket, you breathe black. And in the omnipresent sound of *noheh* mourning chants echoing in the interrogation chambers of *Komiteh Markazi*—as a woman is lashed in the presence of her crying son—you hear a harrowing, ironic black: *Aseman khoun geryeh kon farzand-e Zahra mizanand*—"Shed tears of blood, sky, the child of Zahra is beaten."

One morning at work Z received a call from her husband in Evin. Two years after his arrest, his case had finally gone to trial and his death sentence was issued. He had called to hear her voice for the last time, but wishing to spare her one last night he did not tell her the sentence. Nevertheless she sensed death and broke down at the office. Dragging her two-year-old daughter to Evin the next day, in the irrational hope that they might take pity on the child, she was informed that the sentence had been carried out at dawn.

At that moment, she said, she detested all hope: her own and his. Not that she was afraid—she had spent her years at Evin too. Under extreme physical pain she had learned how what is temporary can be eternal and how even this eternity comes to pass. Enduring the pain but remaining unyielding, her belief was tested and confirmed: the future, change, freedom will triumph. But that morning when she suddenly saw her husband devoured by the beast of the struggle for freedom, everything in her mind vanished but one word: Hamid. Through the days that followed, she felt the sound of his name pounding unrelentingly inside her head, claiming, as it were, the man inside the sacrificial dress.

In prison she had come to know the power to wipe out any existence, temporary or eternal. She had learned to stop the most automatic train of thought. She had stopped herself from thinking about her injuries, wiping from her mind the image of the lacerated and gashed flesh on her feet and legs. Through the long feverish days of her infected wounds she had denied pain, thinking of water, of waves and rivers. But now "Hamid" pounded in her ears. The existence of this pain she was incapable of obliterating. She felt the swelling of a hard, massive rage—a black stone germinating from deep earth—pressing against every fiber. And at a secretly held memorial service for her husband, she sat unmoved through the bitter words of a friend's eulogy:

"Underneath the fields of poppy and tulip the blood shed for liberty and for Islam have dissolved in one another. Let us call 'progress' that which grows on this blood over time. So progress, too, shall become a legacy of the Islamic Republic."

In an opposition group's call for nourishing the tree of liberty, broadcast over unbearable static from Iraq to its followers in Iran, fear of hope creeps under my skin. The broadcast conveys orders to members who may already be breaking under torture, or may not be far from it, or may be recruiting younger brothers and sisters. The voice, authoritative and inexpressive, at times barely discernible, guides me through underground tunnels to small windowless rooms where blood and information will be drawn from me. And I see myself "standing" to write down my life, retreating behind layers of black cloth, standing to prayer five times a day, and waiting in line to report those who break the rules and share their morning tea. I see myself slowly succumbing to the black and pungent magnetic field of God, martyrdom, and relinquished strife.

Sheikh Eshraq

And yet *siyahi*—blackness—is a ploy.
A long-standing National Front member—blindfolded, his hands tied behind his back, in solitary confinement for eight months—knows this. He is close to seventy years old with much prison experience in his lifetime, and while his body may not endure severe beatings, his spirit is virtually indestructible. The effort to break him takes all the ingenuity that the prisons of the Islamic Republic can muster.

They work on disrupting his psychological balance by tampering with his visual and auditory senses and his perception of time. No sound reaches him but the *noheh* chants, on and off erratically for hours at a stretch or sometimes just minutes. "Lunch" is not brought to him for a good twenty-four hours after "breakfast," but it is followed immediately by "supper." Or breakfast may follow lunch and lunch supper. This goes on in a calculatedly unrepeated pattern. But pattern is not something that can be so easily erased from a developed human brain. Sensory awareness and memory discern patterns.

Mr. A listens to the silence patiently, and with time vibrations and faint sounds of footsteps and faraway activity reach him. A shaky regularity emerges to which he sets his internal clock. He practices visualizing the faces of his children and grandchildren. He tries to recollect the architecture of every house in which he has lived. He recites every line of poetry that he knows by heart and memorizes verses of his own composition. He designs book covers and visualizes the most space-efficient layout for articles in the magazine he edited before his arrest. Forms become so vivid in his mind that light is not blinding when his blindfold is taken off after eight months.

It is farce too. Over the years, gray hair and bald spots have slowly modified the pitch-black appearance of brother Pasdars. And oversized black army boots—hand-me-downs from the brothers—sticking out from beneath black chadors and flopping forward with each step have a way of caricaturizing the overall effect of the sisters of Zeynab.

Mr. A said that like squids we throw black ink at our objects of fear and we take refuge in the darkness. "Darkness shelters all sides," he said, and he read to me from Sohrevardi, "Sheikh Eshraq," the 12th century "Illumination" philosopher:

> "Brothers of Truth, shed your skins like the snake sheds his and transgress like the ant who is heard by none. Like the scorpion, carry your weapon behind you, for evil strikes from the back. Partake of poison so you may live well and love death so you truly live. Be in constant flight and make no permanent nest, for all birds are taken from their nests, and if you have no wings to fly with, crawl upon the earth and occupy no permanent space. Be like the ostrich who swallows warm stones and like the buzzard who swallows hard bones and like the salamander who lives in fire, so that you suffer no harm. And like the moth do not come out in daylight so you remain safe from foes."

Being here

As Sheikh Eshraq would have it, the community of arts and letters, for one, has transformed itself into a zoo of sorts. Were I to describe any one creature to any degree of accuracy, however, I would blow his or her cover. I cannot relate the opinion of a particular scholar, or the style of a poet, or the generic nuances of the latest work of a short-story writer, or the timbre of a singer's voice, or the background of any of them without taking a risk at their expense. In a tightly knit community each is well known. Let us just say that some are men, some women, some have work, others no longer do, some are *ancien régime,* some "left," others neither, some have prison experience, some not, some are hopeful, others despairing.

The forces of an unexpectedly calculating strategy of censorship—a *meta*-censorship, one could say—are at work to deny the very existence of this stratum of the Iranian population. The idea is to wipe out any sign of dissent by dismissing both the significance and the existence of it, self-contradictory as the attempt is. The confiscation and monopolization of the basic tools of the trade are the most pragmatic application of this attempt at denial—a far better strategy than the usual time-consuming and face-losing bureaucratic mechanisms of censorship.

Nabsh-e Qabr (exhumation) is the term the Islamic Republic uses to refer to the publication of works by the pre-revolutionary intelligentsia. (The few literary magazines and journals continue to "exhume" the well-known and respected writers of "the past" who happen to have the most number of readers and students. The revolution is, after all, not yet a decade old.) But this is not an attempt at making room for a new generation of intellectuals to flourish—the "new generation" has all too successfully either been nipped in the bud or shipped off abroad. The battle is not generational but ideological. It is any sense of continuity that the Islamic Republic finds threatening.

In a tongue-in-cheek editorial titled "Which Ethics?" in one of the now discontinued literary journals excerpts from a letter by a *Dr. Khodaju* ("Seeker of God") are published:

"Persuaded by a friend," Dr. Khodaju writes, "I picked up a copy of your magazine. I was shocked with what I found. It was as if no revolution had ever taken place: the same old worn out sterile faces... people who once may have had something to say but today are capable of nothing more than whining and complaining."

Dr. Khodaju goes on to denounce by name, and pronounce dead for all practical purposes, many of the writers who to this day lead the Iranian intellectual community. He then contrasts the "complacency" of these intellectuals with the dedication and fervor of revolutionary youth who continue to sacrifice their lives for Islamic struggle. He apparently uses vulgar and offensive words against certain individuals, which the magazine omits.

The editorial board responds to the letter as it best can. It proposes to Dr. Khodaju that for the fruition of the Great Tree of the Revolution more is needed than sheer youthful enthusiasm. It points out that a nation must not ignore its past since the past illuminates the future, and so forth. It quotes at length an incoherent monologue of Dr. Khodaju's on the "passivity" of the notion of *fana* (Sufi "annihilation") and on the activism of "Shiite madness" (here Khodaju quotes from the writings of a "British imperialist"). In closing, the magazine invites comments from readers. Then comes a footnoted postscript in small, ink-stained print:

"We intended to publish Dr. Khodaju's letter in its entirety, so we wrote to invite him to assist us in editing his letter and clearing the text of some discourteous words. The letter we sent to his address was returned to us by the post office. We assigned a colleague to deliver the message in person. No residence was found at Dr. Khodaju's address."

There is a question discreetly raised here: Who exists? A community resisting being buried alive, or "God-seekers" with fancied titles and fake addresses?

The confusion over what there is and what there is not fits in nicely with a society run on a black market economy. "Is" there sufficient food in Iran? Yes, there is. All kinds of commodities not indigenous to Iranian soil, from fresh pineapples to asparagus, are still available. You can still have your filet-kabab, your Johnny Walker Black Label. Milk and cheese and eggs, meat and rice, fruits and vegetables can be found (though usually with a little assistance from your friendly neighborhood grocers). But beyond the meager rations (a hundred grams of butter, two hundred grams of cheese, one liter of milk, per person per month) allowed by each household's basij-notebook, everything must be paid for in the rial equivalent of black-market-exchange-rate dollars.

With the basij-notebook you expect to pay 24 tomans for a kilo of cheese and 30 tomans for a kilo of meat, while in the free market they go for 240 and 300 tomans per kilo. The explanation for this is that imported items are paid for by the wholesaler in the black-market (sometimes called "free-market" by the officials, depending on the exigencies of the moment) exchange rate that fluctuates at between fifteen and twenty times the official rate. No matter that milk and eggs are not imported; prices are adjusted to the black market dollar anyway. The only exception is bread—that most symbolic of all foodstuff. Bread is the only subsidized item and is kept at a low price. Bakeries are ordered to display their store of flour in clear public sight, in tribute to plentitude and a humane economy. "Shortage," then, does not accurately describe the situation.

The paper "shortage" is one of the most enduring shortages. Not only paper's dollar-based price but government-imposed "priority" projects act as qualifiers for the word.

As the summer of 1986 drew to a close and the publishing industry continued its near total halt in printing anything not essentially Islamic propaganda, people speculated that there might not be enough paper for the annual publication of textbooks. Hand-me-down textbooks became hot commodities. Children were told that they would have to observe strict quotas in notebook consumption. Already most children were being sent to school half-time as a result of the growing population of Tehran and not enough schools and teachers. This is especially true of the lowest-income areas of Tehran where each school day is divided into the morning and the afternoon shifts. There is continual talk of the possibility of reducing the number of subjects as a means of saving classroom space, teacher time, and, by eliminating the textbooks and homework for those subjects, paper.

On the other hand, the abundant, high-priority publications of the Islamic Republic are displayed in newsstands all around the country. At one quarter of the price of a bastard (by choice) literary magazine printed on yellowish "strawpaper," magazines such as *Pasdar-e Islam* (a publication of the Qom Islamic Propaganda Center) take their regular prominent spots at the newsstands every week.

The front cover is usually the only page of these magazines that is perused by the passers-by—a montage of the Allah emblem of the Islamic Republic rising from the black stone of the *ka'ba* like a full moon, or some action photograph of smiling boys with *Ya Sarollah* headbands on their way to the front. The back cover, expressing a more reflective moment, often displays a quotation from the Koran in *nasta'liq* calligraphy, embellished by loose-ended curves and open loops of imitation *eslimi* ornamentation, punctuated with come-from-nowhere tiny three-petalled flowers.

What surely goes unnoticed by the majority of the reading public, however, is the *de luxe* and *glacé* paper and the generous layout of the articles contained between the covers. The attendant of one newspaper kiosk told me that these magazines are collected, almost wholly unsold, by their distributors when the new issues appear. Paper recycling being a thriving industry, he said that they probably end up as cardboard for confectionery boxes.

The new oral tradition

Underground and without paper, the Iranian intellectual community has been forced into a new oral tradition. Private gatherings—parties, dinners, all-night sessions of poetry, music, discussion, or instruction—are the venues of this tradition. Typically the most personal thoughts and the most rigorous learning are imparted by the same person at the same sitting.

To describe these exchanges I could conjure up a memory of steaming inside my Islamic uniform in the heat of a July afternoon in a bare university classroom where I talked to a professor of Persian literature. He smiled at my nationalist sentiments as he respectfully nodded to his bearded or black-veiled students who eyed me with hostility and him with distrust. I can remember the tall woman poet always in black who said: *Mard-e Irani zan ra bavar nadarad*—"The Iranian man does not believe in woman." Or I can recall a certain singer, now in her prime, who sang for us at a dinner party with an uncommon serenity stemming from resignation to the fact that by the time female voice is allowed to be broadcast, commercially recorded, or heard in public, it will probably be too late for her. I can recall the long "Ode to the Future" of a poet not in the habit of composing *qasidas,* who sees the progress of Iran in the hands of its women and who trusts his new work only to his memory.

I could write of the hard-to-interpret sparkle deep inside the tired eyes of one of the last great old men of Persian Letters as he advised me to abandon my studies in literature: "Those interests belonged to another time. This is a different world now." Or I could write of a streak of violence in the soft words and quiet spectacle of an up-and-coming playwright. Or I might shuffle the details of words and characters, or invent them, lest I jeopardize any individual. To sketch a community so that no real-life individual can be traced, one inevitably slips into fiction.

The evenings I spent in Tehran are interwoven in my memory into one long, animated night. In spite of the constant threat of an ambush by the Pasdars of the local komiteh, this is when life surfaces from its daytime hiding places. In smaller apartment complexes—the larger ones are patrolled by the resident hezbollahi families stationed there by the government—little children are taught to be on the watch for approaching komiteh vehicles. When one is sighted, the group of little children playing together disperses in all directions. Doorbells are rung in alarm and guests frantically bustle about flushing alcoholic beverages down the toilet, hiding records and cassettes or musical instruments, and throwing on the hejab.

But the evening has a way of remaining concentrated and coherent with a desperate vitality brewing in every corner. One might overhear, for instance, an impromptu lecture at a busy dinner table:

"It is the business of revolutions to murder God. In 1793, for example, God was beheaded in the person of Louis XVI. But our situation was different. We had no representation of divinity. It was impossible to attribute *farr-e izadi* to the son of Reza Khan Mirpanj, the cossack mercenary installed on the throne by the British. In order for our revolution to claim its legitimacy, God had to be embodied and killed elsewhere—in the person of each martyr perhaps. I don't believe that it is that little key to heaven dangling from their necks that inspires these young men to sacrifice their lives. It must be the cry of *Anal Haq* that rings in their hearts: *I am the Truth*... Who would have thought that the legacy of Hallaj could have such political contemporary application?"

Or I might be talking to a friend of a friend, reminiscing on where I was the winter of 1979 when the revolution triumphed: "To think that we celebrated... that friends came over with champagne by the case and we went on our rampage of ecstatic long-distance phone calls, that nice, clear California night! I only wonder, how could it...? How could *we*...?" My friend laughed. "How *we* could is simple. Since when does humankind look past the climax?"

Over a glass of tea, a composer "cleansed" from his job might relate:

"I dreamed that it rained a slow, steady rain. It started as a drizzle and we expected it to evaporate before reaching the ground. But it persisted, and, disbelievers as we have become, we walked around holding out our palms and looking up suspiciously at the sky. The rain did not stop and we took shelter when it started pouring. We watched as it washed off the slogans scribbled on walls and windows. We watched it wash the Friday Prayer markings off the streets around the university. We watched it crumble and wash away the hideous concrete overpasses of Tehran and all the dusty, unmaintained cars crawling on them. The rain spread and slowly undermined the foundations of the decrepit luxury villas on the Caspian coast and carried off the debris in a flood. It muffled and extinguished the flames covering the surface of the earth in Khuzestan. It washed off the tar. It washed off the blood."

The party

The famous translator SK and his wife are at the party. It is late in the evening and as the last of the host's supply of homemade *araq* is relentlessly attacked we listen to SK's tribulations in his most recent project: translating T.S. Eliot for publication in an unforeseeable future.

He suddenly turns to me. "And what is it that you—daughter of a translator, come from America—want to do?"

I say that I want to write. "I grew up on translation and have been living in translation since I left Iran. I'm tired of translations."

He asks what I am working on, and I explain that I hope to make an article out of the notes I have been taking on my trip.

"If you want to communicate with English speakers you have to use the language they understand, right?" he asks.

I agree.

"I will help you," he says. "Try this on Iran," and he quotes in English from T.S. Eliot:

> *The eyes are not here*
> *There are no eyes here*
> *In this valley of dying stars*
> *In this hollow valley*
> *This broken jaw of our lost kingdoms*

He pauses to take a sip of his drink. Then he asks, "Will you write about someone like me?"

I say that perhaps I should.

"Then write that this is my message—the message of a

drunk old Iranian translator, clawing, to the best of his ability, the insides of the belly of the Islamic Republic"—and he quotes from Eliot again:

> *Not for me the martyrdom, the ecstasy of thought and prayer*
> *Not for me the ultimate vision.*

As the sour-cherry Vishnovka is brought in, he pours himself another drink. "Go forth, daughter, and translate," his son mocks him. SK tastes the Vishnovka with concentration, compliments the hostess on the liqueur's perfect degree of sweetness, ignores his son, and continues on a more sober note.

"Translation is a practice too humble for most people. The work itself, when it is successful, becomes obsolete the moment it is read. The reader, having taken one step toward understanding something foreign is immediately ready for the next step—and this frustrates the sophisticated reader. In the west, he blames translation for coming between himself and the original work, and given the inevitability of this mediation he is likely to give up in a huff. He is impatient to go directly, somehow magically, to the heart of the matter—as Goethe thought he did with Hafez. Or, rarely, he may recognize a kindred wit and run with it—as Voltaire did with Sa'di.

"But for the most part the western reader does not, *will not,* accept the idea of translation. It is inconceivable to him that things—especially if they come from the east—can only become accessible in degrees. No, he wants all or nothing. It's quite imperialistic really... Add the fact that the east is only recognized when it is *exotic*—which means inaccessible and implicitly erotic—and we can guess at the violence that this inspires: take things by force, violate, conquer... But then God forbid that our words ring familiar—then we surely must be *westernized*."

"Westernization...,"someone barges in. "The only thing that really means is that we speak their language and they don't speak ours."

"I think there are two solutions to the problem—at least as far as the literary world is concerned," SK goes on. "First, do let us forget about *texts*. My generation of translators did not translate *texts*. In our innocence we merely translated life and death and all that comes in between—as expressed in foreign words. You may want to call it writing but this is what needs to be translated *from* our language now. Second—and forgive me for saying so myself—the translator must be reckoned with. We are neither native-informants nor proselytes of any sort. Readers, interpreters, mediators, *we* are the problems of translation."

Then he turns to me. "And you had better not get tired of translation so soon. You still have less choice than you think."

SK's wife has been fidgeting for a while. At her own house, once she has cleared the dinner table, she might be persuaded to bring out her notebook and read her own poetry. But now she has decided that her husband has drunk enough and is worried about the alcohol on his breath if they are stopped at a Revolutionary Guard checkpoint on their way home.

"It is not necessary to give the situation such epic dimensions," she says by way of wrapping up the conversation. "I think there is an invisible little difference at work here. There is a fundamental incongruity in aesthetics... Forget about genuinely foreign things; western art likes to make even familiar things strange. This is no secret—it's all over their literary theory. And we are—Iranians are—just the opposite. We go to any length to make foreign things our own. We even name our sons after Alexander, Genghiz Khan, and Tamerlane— those most brutal conquerors of our country. For us nothing is sweeter than setting eyes on the familiar: *Bashad ke baz binim didar-e ashena ra.* This is how in our poetry the Great Unknown is beckoned near... but we must be going now."

The line is a famous one from Hafez: "Would it that we may set eyes on the familiar one again."

She, MM, perhaps one of the best Iranian poets writing at present, does not publish. SK recites her poetry and she edits his translations, but she refuses to publish. Earlier, as she pored over someone's new Robert Frost acquisition, I thought I saw a smile flicker across her face when she read the lines: "Love at the lips was touch / As sweet as I could bear..."

SK has his own interpretation.

"It is as if there is a sleep from which she doesn't want to be awakened." And then he can't help paraphrasing Eliot: "She fears that human voices will wake her and she will drown."

In preparation for leaving, MM disappears inside her Islamic garb and produces a few cardamom pods from her purse. I learn that cardamom seeds work well for camouflaging the smell of alcohol on the breath.

"Don't be deceived by her lyric spirit," says SK as he stumbles to the door, popping the seeds in his mouth. "She is so resourceful she would make an excellent double agent."

Later, lying in bed at dawn and watching the outline of the Alborz range emerging from the dark, I have the vision that we have collected our belongings and are sleepwalking out of our old family house when the dormant volcano, our majestic Mount Damavand, erupts. The explosion floods us with light as we freeze in mid-flight. Dazed and awakened in various degrees, we retrace our steps, set down our things, and settle once more.

Azadeh

On my last night in Tehran, an unusually humid summer evening, my uncle and I were on our way to a friend's house. Driving through the dark and deserted streets where the lights have been dimmed or turned off since the first bombing raid of six years ago, we pulled over to buy cigarettes from a blind peddler. He counted out the change without needing to step in front of the headlights of the car to see what he was doing. I had been thinking of a friend of mine who wondered whether we were going to Iran that summer in order to say our goodbyes. I was thinking that I should remember to tell her not to fret over needing to say goodbye. One does not take leave of things; things take leave of one.

My uncle and I were the only members of our immediate families in Iran at the time. Our extended family is not atypical now in being scattered around the globe, in search of asylum and who knows what else. The family members remaining in Iran represent all the rest, and one often finds oneself having inherited roles and relationships of the missing members. I had suddenly, and very pleasantly, found myself a friend to the friends of each of my parents. I wondered if the logic behind displacement, misplacement, and replacement will ever be accessible to us.

As we turned into our friend's street we drove by a large stone house that was hit during the bombing raid of the past spring. The rubble was neatly swept from the street back into the courtyard and left there.

In the study of my father's friend, Mr. H, I leaned against

the *jajim*-covered pillows on the rug, around a brazier of hot coals keeping the tea warm. The ladies sat on the sofa, crossing their stockinged legs, and watched. I talked books and literature and theory with the men as Mr. H dug under the ashes for a red coal to hold against a little chunk of fragrant Mahan opium for me. I was instructed to blow gently on the coal until it glowed under its coat of ash and the opium barely sizzled. Then I inhaled slowly and deeply.

"Enough of this hysteria over the Great Satan, imperialism at large, or as they say, The Empire…" Mr. H was saying.

I held my breath.

"Formalism is a viable choice—remember the Russians—when a revolution comes along to awaken us from the nightmare of history," he advised me.

Mr. P, a political scientist turned art historian, smiled. "Let us say it momentarily disrupts the nightmare."

Azadeh, the five-year-old daughter of Mr. H, climbed on the couch and snuggled between her mother and aunt. The women were looking at photographs that Mrs. H had taken at the tomb of Sheikh Safi in Azarbaijan, discussing the patterns of the mosaic. Mrs. P said it was wonderful that the Iranian so-called Arabesque with its linear play flourished in spite of the invasion of the Arab florals and the geometric patterns of Central Asia. While Mrs. H stroked her daughter's hair and reevaluated her photographs, the little girl fell asleep in her lap.

As the conversation of the men turned to copyright laws and editors' fees, I walked over to Mr. H's desk. I looked at the group engrossed in their talk, leaning against the pillows with their forearms resting on their knees. I savored the moment of artificially induced sense of tranquility. Mr. P overturned his tea on the rug while reaching for the sugar. When my glance returned to the desk I flipped through one of the books that were lying open there, a history of the final days of the Third Reich with black and white photographs of Dresden, Berlin, and Frankfurt after the bombardments.

On the cover was a picture of a telegraph pole standing in a devastated street with pieces of paper tacked onto it with the whereabouts of neighborhood survivors.

When Mr. H carried his daughter upstairs to bed, his two sons were watching a television interview with Rafsanjani, the Speaker of the Parliament. Rafsanjani spoke with his usual smirk:

"We have nothing to fear from the U.S. in the Persian Gulf. Their political system is too disembodied and much too stricken with internal opposition to be capable of carrying out any decisive policy in the Gulf."

The boys, both near draft age, watched with anxious attention.

"We are prepared to continue this war for another twenty years if we need to," Rafsanjani declared.

When dinner was served the boys walked off with their plates to eat by themselves in front of the turned-off television set.

The evening ended during the daily power outage with an unlikely thunderstorm. As we all watched from the porch, the great khaki-colored clay pots holding the swaying Yas plants turned dark brown in the rain. And as one of the ladies ran down to collect the fragrant little white flowers strewn about, each one of us, I know, prayed for survival.

Sorry, friends

With their mission of destruction
Prophets came to our century.
Ceaseless explosions
And noxious clouds,
Are these echoes of sacred texts?
When you reach the moon—
my friend, my brother, my blood-tie—
Write the history of the massacre of flowers.

Forough Farrokhzad wrote these lines in 1966.

On Sunday, September 20, 1987, Neusha Farrahi, 31, poured gasoline over his body and set himself on fire to protest the visit of the president of Iran, Ali Khamenei, to the United Nations. This occurred in Los Angeles at a demonstration against the Iran-Iraq war.

I went to elementary school with Neusha. He was a passionate and conflicted little boy. I remember looking away from him whenever he fixed his knotted gaze on me from behind his blond curls. I never saw him as an adult but I knew he had become a left-leaning writer. I suspect that his historical materialism fought a losing battle with his first-hand experience of the way in which history changes nothing. After the fire he was unable to talk and I did not write to him, knowing that he was surrounded with love and attention. I was thinking of his long, painful, and possibly lonely recovery and how the support of long-lost friends would be most useful then. He died two weeks later.

The picture of Neusha's charred body was on the cover of the *New York Post* the day after his immolation. This was no serene image of a Buddhist monk in flames protesting in Vietnam. Neusha lay on the pavement like a crumpled piece of paper. The *Los Angeles Times* reported the incident with the obscure headline: "Man sets self on fire to protest Iranian's visit." Other "serious" newspapers neither covered this incident nor the many similar anti-war protests taking place around the country.

Around the same time, the captured Iranian sailors from the *Iran Ajr,* caught laying mines in the Persian Gulf, were returned by American authorities to Iran—despite their cooperation with the Americans in locating the mines, and despite their request for asylum because of their uncertain fate in Iran after that cooperation. Nor did this incident capture in any major newspaper more than a passing mention tucked away far from the front page.

Iran, in spite of all efforts however desperate or ill-fated, is persistently portrayed by images that the Islamic Republic determines: blindfolded American hostages, masses of zealous, slogan-spouting "believers," the dark and mesmerizing eyes of the Imam peering beneath his permanent frown.

One of the anti-war demonstrations was organized in New York City a week before Khamenei's UN visit by a small ad-hoc group comprised mostly of opposition activists of the Shah era. Figuring that a strong visual impact was the only way to capture a split-second of much-hoped-for television news coverage, the group discussed producing two images: one an effigy of Khomeini set on fire and the second a copy of the Koran in flames. The second idea was controversial. There was fear of offending "true" believers and although the primary receivers of this image would ideally and realistically be the American public (via the media) and a limited number of people in Iran (via word of mouth), it was difficult to assess the reaction that would be evoked.

But an even more important question was this: "Given the strong connection between fascism and the image of book-burning, do we think we can sever that connection and link our own book-burning to a message of struggle against Islamic fascism?" Having reached no decision, the group carried both an effigy of Khomeini and a voluminous edition of the Koran to the demonstration. I joined them that day.

On September 23, while Neusha lay sedated but fully conscious in intensive care, fire was foremost on many of our minds. The idea of book burning finally ruled out, however, the large Koran in its fluorescent green cover sat on the sidewalk. The plan was to burn the effigy of Khomeini as the pro-Khomeini demonstrators marched down First Avenue past our small group in makeshift paper face masks. A few minutes before the march the police informed us that they were not prepared to give us protection against the "seven hundred animals"—the supporters of the Islamic Republic—coming our way. With the Hezbollah once again in the spotlight, this time by managing to bully NYPD, it was *our* demonstration permit that was revoked.

Clubs, switch-blades, and broken bottles are the weapons of the Hezbollah in street confrontations. We don't carry these things. We did not stay.

Kashf-e Hejab

2007–2008

Kashf-e Hejab

On 17th of Dey, 1314 (January 7, 1935) by order of Reza Shah Pahlavi, all Iranian women were to shed their hejab. The day was known as the day of *kashf-e hejab*, the "revealing" of the veil.

A few years ago I recorded some conversations with a friend of my father's, Mr. Marashi, who recounted some of the historic events he had witnessed in his life. The day of kashf-e hejab was one. At an assembly for a number of Tehran high schools, Reza Shah made an appearance flanked by his de-veiled wife and daughters. "We stood in orderly lines listening to the Shah," said Mr. Marashi. "Boys on one side and girls on the other..." Reza Shah gave a rousing speech, reminding the young people of their responsibility for building the future of the country. "We were a little awed by the presence of the Shah and his family, but we weren't listening to what he was saying," Mr. Marashi remembered. "We were much more interested in the pretty girls standing a few feet away from us."

Those girls would be our mothers. On that historic day they stood in lady-like dignity with their single or double braids falling down the back of their school uniforms. They did their best to ignore the boys.

After kashf-e hejab policemen were under orders to snatch any kind of covering off women's heads in the streets. Many men forbade their womenfolk to leave their houses and many women refused to do so of their own accord. It was a brutish, top-down royal decree, typical of Reza Shah. I am perfectly capable of seeing the undemocratic nature of this decree and

I do understand the class implications of it. But, in my heart of hearts, was I ever bothered by it?

No. Even my grandmothers were not bothered by it.

In my family there was only one *ammeh-khanom*, sister of my paternal grandfather, who refused to go out without her chador after kashf-e hejab. The scene of another ammeh-khanom's encounter with the police *agent* who ordered her to take off her scarf was laughingly enacted in my family for years. "And – here – is – to – the – health – of – his – Pahlavi – Majesty…" she had enunciated, slowly peeling the hejab off her head. She was well pleased with a performance that had evoked chuckles in the onlookers.

My mother and aunts and all the braid-heads in Mr. Marashi's memory took kashf-e hejab as a matter of course. They had never worn the hejab as children and by their adolescence it was already banned. But women were not the only ones whose appearance was changing. Men were also switching to western clothes and shaved faces—after all, the boys at that 17th of Dey ceremony were not exactly attired in traditional Iranian garb either. The appearance-overhaul of the country had been well under way by that time. Mud and cobble-stoned streets were paved. Automobiles drove on them. Electricity transformed days and nights. Life was changing fast and looking different.

Still, in Mr. Marashi's recollection, there was novelty in the sight of hundreds of unveiled school girls, attempting a dignified appearance between giggle attacks. Though many boys were accustomed to seeing their sisters, cousins, and friends without veils, the bounty had never been quite as vast as it spread before their eyes on that momentous day. Many of those ogling boys ended up marrying the officially de-veiled young ladies in their neighboring rows. As it turned out, those uniformed girls throwing side-glances at their male counterparts made regular wives and mothers and generally lived without debauchery. And many of them accomplished a great deal more for their country. The Islamic Republic knows this very well.

The kashf-e hejab decree was certainly dramatic. It was a most visible manifestation of profound and far-reaching social change. As the word "kashf" implies, it was indeed a kind of revelation: It *revealed* the presence of women in Iranian society. By endorsing that presence it expanded the role of women and increased their significance. But kashf-e hejab was not the moment that set the clock ticking on the emancipation of Iranian women. The "liberation" of women was part of a wider movement for democratization that had gained momentum in the nineteenth century. The notions of freedom and equality were the cornerstones of the Iranian battle for sovereignty (remember colonialism?) and democracy. Scores of writers and activists were engaged in "awakening" the nation, as they called it, to the modern world. Printing presses were spitting out ink-smeared original and translated publications at full capacity. Young Iranians went to Europe to study. Modern science was thrilling and technological advance irresistible. After the victory of the Constitutional Revolution in 1905, especially, there was no turning back.

But democracy, "high" culture, science, and technology were not the only appeal of the modern world. Thanks to the latest technology, western popular culture burst upon Iranian society and was embraced with relish. The glimpse into western society provided by translations of novels was in time projected onto cinema screens. Even the most obscure characters in novels or silent movies were closely observed for attire, behavior, mores, and what have you. From high to popular culture, from Montesquieu to Greta Garbo, the lure of the west left its imprint. By the 1930s the heads of some of the most driven Iranians had already been filled with what had made the west powerful and rich. And it would be silly to deny that catching up with the accomplished and glamorous west was a consuming ambition for a significant number of Iranians. By the time the 17th of Dey came along, for far too many people to be ideologized away by the Islamic Republic, the lifting of a piece of cloth off women's heads was just that.

But now here we are, 73 years later, and many of the

grand-daughters of the braid-heads of 1935 have never been in public with uncovered heads. Starting in 1979, layers were added step by step to required women's clothing: headscarves, long pants, thick socks, chador, *rupoush, manteau, maqna'eh,* and so forth. If Reza Shah's royal decree was enforced by veils being snatched off women's heads and ripped on the spot, the religious decree after the revolution has been enforced by flogging, jail, throwing acid in the face, and other gross barbarisms. I don't know what the ultimate penalty is for refusing to abide by the Islamic dress code. I don't know if anyone has ever received the ultimate penalty—it is easy enough to throw a piece of cloth over someone's head and save her life.

What a catastrophe. What nonsense.

"Do you have to wear *that thing* when you go to Iran?"

For close to thirty years I have been asked that question. It is a highly annoying one. Is it equally fascinating whether Indian women, or men for that matter, wear saris or kurtas back home? Why this concern over how I cover myself? We all cover our bodies somehow, depending on where we are. What people who ask this question don't realize is that most of us cringe at this concern over the clothing of Iranian women. It directs an unwelcome kind of gaze towards us. Walking down the street in my nondescript attire, the last thing I want is to attract attention to how my body is clad—here, there, or anywhere. (And I won't even mention the patronizing overtones of the question.)

But we have the Islamic Republic to thank for this unwelcome gaze, as much as the limits of western experience and imagination. If Reza Shah *de-veiled* Iranian women, the Islamic Republic subjected them all over to the *unveiling* of which old Victorian obscenity, for one, was so fond. We are now subjected to everybody and their brother—and sister—commenting on how and how much we cover our bodies. The phenomenon begs for endless body-politic analyses. Dissertations beg to be written and careers to be made. But apart from annoyance there is nothing in it for the average Iranian woman walking to the grocery store, inside or outside Iran.

There certainly has been a change during Ahmadinejad's presidency. That nasty note of vigilance has been reintroduced into the enforcement of hejab. The young woman sitting next to me on the plane before landing in Tehran advised me to change the long shirt I got away with last time I visited in 2005. There were certainly less outrageous outfits on the streets and more patrolling of young people's hangouts. I had read personal accounts of all this and seen pictures and YouTube clips of harassment of women before my trip. Even a number of men's barber shops had been shut down. I was not quite so cavalier about my attire this year.

And yet, I had an irrational and nagging feeling that something is close to coming to an end in Iran. There is hardly any evidence to support this, but I have a feeling that another *kashf-e hejab* is imminent.

The kind of Muslim I am

I have a cousin in Istanbul who is a devout Muslim. Despite his severe hearing and vision impairments he has held a job conscientiously and without a break since his family emigrated to Turkey after the revolution. Years ago my grandmother, herself hardly religious and married to a decidedly unreligious man, guided him to having faith. It has served him well. He is just about the holiest person I know, and not because he says prayers every day and fasts the entire month of Ramezan. He harbors no grudge against his fate.

When I arrived in Istanbul on my way to Tehran, Ramezan (that's "Ramadan" in Persian pronunciation) had already begun. The *azan*, the call to prayer, rang out diligently from the neighborhood mosques three times a day. Solitary sentinels walked the streets an hour before sunrise, beating their drums to wake people up for their early morning meal. Near *eftar*, the evening breaking of the fast, driving got particularly hairy as people edgy with hunger rushed home. I decided to fast a day in honor of my cousin. I like the breaking of the fast with a glass of tea and dates, and I wanted to share that moment with him.

Years ago, a year before the revolution, I had gone back to Iran for the summer as a student. Having been in the U.S. for a couple of years, I had developed some distance and tolerance for religious rituals. Perhaps I was also a little affected by the alternately romanticized and politically charged version of Islam right before the revolution. That was the only other time I fasted. My grandmother's cozy cottage by the Caspian Sea also had something to do with it. I spent a sweet afternoon with her as she showed me how to cook halva on her primus "Alladin" stove. We broke our fasts together with tea and fresh halva under the shade on her veranda. I had just as sweet a moment breaking our fasts together with my cousin in Istanbul.

I also think well of the practice of Muslim prayers. It is a mild and effective form of yoga, complete with breathing regulated through recitations, resting in a variation of the child's pose in *sojoud,* and sensible stretches. I particularly appreciate the hands placed above the knees as you bend at the hip joints in *rokou* and exhale; it stretches the hamstrings without straining the lower back. It is a very good thing to do five times a day. The physical sensations of fasting are pleasant too. It has a calming, introverting effect, especially if you don't have to cope with the demands of jobs and other stresses. At the end of the day you are generally more thirsty than hungry. A glass of freshly brewed tea with the first dates of the season tastes really divine.

And that's just about all I get out of the pieties of Islam.

"Oh, no… you're going to be in Tehran at Ramezan," is how my friends in Iran reacted when I told them about my trip. "Can't you come some other time?"

I was mildly curious to be in Iran during Ramezan. It turned out to be quite as inconvenient as I was warned. No restaurants are open during the day, which means no lunch dates without putting someone to the trouble of cooking. Eating and drinking is strictly prohibited in public from sunrise to sunset. As my friend Marjan, who is normally quite brazen in breaking rules, and I walked about one day, even she appeared a little nervous sneaking little bites of the bread we carried in our pockets. When we got thirsty she took me to the shop of a Jewish antique dealer of her acquaintance. "Iraj Khan, help!" she said. "We need some tea." Iraj Khan dutifully closed his shop door and produced for us glasses of tea with *gol-gavzaban,* which was apparently a specialty of his. We drank a couple of glasses each, chatted, and left without buying anything from the poor man.

Getting around the inconveniences of Ramezan is not that hard, but what got to me was the fasting of people I had never known to be religious. The somber declining of food and drink, the pious halo around the neatly knotted head scarf, the morning nap after staying up to observe the night of *ahya* ("The *what* of Yahya?" my brazen friend asked), the maternal bliss lighting up women's faces while feeding their hungry and ill-tempered grown sons—this was nearly enough to ruin the sweetness of my *eftar* with my cousin.

But even I, grown up with zero religious reverence and identity, have become defensive over being Muslim in the U.S. I don't look particularly Iranian (I'm not dark), have an American husband, and don't speak English with a heavy accent. It is easy for people to adopt an "I don't mean you…" attitude with me. Black people in America know about this. But the version I receive is tinged with the piety of liberal America, the latter day white man's burden. Halos glow over people's heads as they seek my engagement in shedding tears over the lot of Muslim women. *Everybody knows* what creeps Muslim men are ("I don't mean *your* family…"). Aren't *we* lucky to live here?

When my son was in first grade a Palestinian-American classmate of his fasted the entire month of Ramadan. The boy's mother was quick to explain to the school that this was entirely the child's decision and he was under no pressure at home. I myself was quite impressed with such discipline exhibited by a six-year old. But of course *everybody knows* that not eating all day is *so bad* for a child. I was regularly drawn into confidences that not only spoke of the little boy with disapproval but with distaste—for Muslims, Arabs, and especially Palestinians. But of course it was in the name of concern over the child's well-being. Didn't I agree: *He can't concentrate? He has no energy?* I was spending time at school but had not noticed much of that. The kid did look a bit frayed by the end of the day but was otherwise fine. It was particularly amusing for me to hear him being talked of as having "impulse control issues." I'll be damned if I don't consider fasting for a month a demonstration of impulse control. Learning to delay gratification does wonders for building self-confidence.

A number of years ago the nine-year-old daughter of a very unreligious Iranian friend of mine in the U.S. also decided to fast for Ramadan. The girl was going through a family crisis and it appeared to me that fasting gave her a sense of control over her life. Recently she explained to me that she had also just moved from a white private school to a multi-ethnic public school and discovered that it was cool to be different. My American stepson decided to become a vegetarian at the age of ten and later a vegan for somewhat similar reasons, I would venture.

In London I saw a t-shirt that said, "Don't panic. I'm Islamic." No Muslim would dream of wearing that in the U.S.

At Darakeh

Darakeh used to be a tiny village in the north of Tehran but is now absorbed into the metropolis. It is above Evin Valley in the foothills on the climb to Mount Tochal, and still maintains its character of a base camp complete with snack vendors and tea houses serving kabab and *dizi*. It is the kind of place where you sit out in the open air on wooden platforms covered with scratchy rugs, and lean against bolsters stuffed with jute. The night I went there with my friend Marjan, groups of young people lounged under the waxing moon of Ramezan, huddled over the electric water-pipe warmers, drinking tea. Quite a few groups included women smoking *qalyoun* (water pipe) which is tolerated off and on by the authorities.

One of the interesting things about Marjan is that a couple of years before the revolution, when young people were leaving Iran in droves, she moved back to Iran from the U.S. She was barely twenty and had spent years in a British boarding school before going to college in Southern California. She never regretted her decision to return and even in the darkest days of the revolution she did not lose her spunk. When hejab became compulsory she took to wearing a version of the mullahs' *'aba,* their cloak, as her over-dress. She still wears those and her mother has become such an expert in sewing them that many a fashionable woman now special orders them from her.

Despite her natural spunk and high spirit Marjan did have some breakdowns over the years. Once after being dragged to the *komiteh* over an infringement of some Islamic technicality she was so frightened by a particularly nasty guard

Kashf-e Hejab

that she broke into sobs, begging to be released. "I haven't done anything. I'm innocent," she said. The guard hissed in her face, "No one is innocent. Even my lord Ali is not innocent"—at which point she really panicked. Her biggest meltdown was at the gate of Evin prison, down the hill from where we had dinner at Darakeh, into which her father had disappeared with no explanation. On that day she became delirious with hysteria, screaming incoherently, and had to be dragged home. But you wouldn't know any of this to look at her. She is very funny.

In the summers she wears a long headscarf made of a very light cotton material. In single ply the gauzy fabric is see-through, so to make it adequately opaque she doubles it. While we were driving earlier that day, we had an encounter with a carload of *entezamat* hejab enforcers. Marjan's scarf had slipped back a bit while driving, showing some hair. Suddenly a patrol car materialized on our trail. "Pull it down," they called to her, motioning to her hejab: "Pull it down." She nodded to them politely, undid the folded part of her scarf and pulled it down to cover not just the exposed part of her hair but her entire face. She continued driving unperturbed with what looked from a distance like a sack over her head. The officers, partly worried and partly amused, kept on following us, flashing their headlights and wildly gesticulating. "Pull it up. Pull it up...," they yelled this time. Even law enforcement is not without entertainment value for Marjan.

People can't resist being drawn into her absurd pranks. She can put on a wickedly innocent act. One of her funniest is taking on a maternal front that attracts mamma's boys, the spoilt ones who think that all women suffer from unconditional maternal regard for them. She often does that for the amusement of the young women accompanying these guys, who usually catch on quick and have a laugh at their expense too.

After our dinner at Darakeh, Marjan struck up a conversation with two very young men drinking tea on the platform next to us. They both had shiny black hair slicked down with globs of gel and one of them was drop-dead gorgeous. Testing the waters for amusement potential we actually got distracted into a conversation with them. The boys had every bit of the dissatisfied-westernized-youth look so we were somewhat shocked to hear that they had fasted all day. They divulged that they had both fasted the entire month of Ramezan since toddlerhood. I listened to them describing the serenity of the breaking of the fast with their families and was sorry to feel the intimacy of my own *eftars* eroding, but no matter... They were sincere young men.

Marjan asked them how fasting as small children was different from fasting as adults. "It starts with having belief," the less gorgeous one said, "and leads to having faith." Later that night, lying awake in bed, I tried to understand this comment. I have no trouble with the part that one could believe fasting is good, but I am completely in the dark as to how one jumps from that belief into the conclusion "...therefore God." I suppose this is the leap of faith that people talk about.

I had to spend a few days taking care of some paperwork for my parents at a government retirement office. At some point, waiting for a piece of paper to be stamped by one official before taking it to another, I had to sit in an office for a while. On the wall above the head of one of the officials were a number of inspirational quotes. I particularly liked the fluffy religiosity of this one: "Don't tell your God what great problems you have. Tell your problems what a great God you have." It struck me that it was not very reassuring for the poor souls sitting and waiting for their problems to be solved by that particular official. As I copied the phrase down in my little notebook, the official in question, a young man with trimmed beard, threw a side glance at what I was doing. Had he started a conversation with me I would have told him what I thought. I thought this particular leap of faith absolves God of all responsibility—even any exertion—and sure seems like a good deal for the almighty. While his subjects are doing all the work, God takes a vacation. "God, therefore you're on your own" does not make much sense, and "God, therefore do whatever you want to others," is quite awful.

The truth is that this religious hopscotch, skipping from random belief to prefabricated faith, is not without consequence for the rest of us. While the faithful are having their day making these leaps, we are being jerked around like marionettes on a string: Eat, Don't eat. Pull up, Pull down. We do our best to keep up but when these yanks on the strings come to the point of "Live, Die" behind closed doors at Evin, we break down.

As we were preparing to leave Darakeh, one of the young men finally overcame his shyness to be so presumptuous as to ask his elders a personal question. "Do you fast?" he asked us. Marjan suddenly turned more serious than she had been all night. "No," she said after the slightest hesitation. "And I don't lie, steal, and hurt other people either. I think that should be enough."

Deathbeds real and imagined

My father died in California four months before my trip to Iran. In the last few months of his life the efforts of reading and writing were almost too much for him. The last books he read were his own unpublished manuscripts. At age 82 he found what he wrote in his sixties "dogmatic" and "naïve." It delighted me that he remained sharp and unsentimental to the end. It also made me laugh about how it takes Middle East politics to make an eighty-year old find his sixty-year old self naïve.

Watching my father surrounded by his manuscripts on his deathbed I was reminded of Rousseau reading his own books at the end of his life. I thought of the good fortune of being able to look back at life through your own writing and how obsessed I have always been about trying to imagine the deathbeds of writers. I can picture Jane Austen burning in a high fever asking her sister to destroy everything but the fiction, published or unpublished. But I have also often fantasized about the deathbeds of the two most powerful men in recent Iranian history: the Shah and Khomeini.

My only personal encounter with the Shah was when in my early youth I bumped into him at the lodge at the newly established Dizin ski resort. I had been in the bathroom while security cleared the lodge for the royal entourage and as I opened the door into the restaurant I collided with His Majesty. I looked up into his face as he steadied me on my feet wobbling in my unbuckled ski boots. There must have been a photo shoot in progress because his face was powdered. I also thought his eyebrows were touched up and there was a hint of a line outside his lower eyelids. "I just bumped into the Shah," I breathlessly reported to my friends, running out as quickly as I could. "He was wearing makeup!"

For whatever reason, my fantasy of the Shah's deathbed is a family scene. I imagine him asking his wife's forgiveness for humiliating her as a wife and under-rating her as a partner. I imagine him advising her not to trust anyone, spend money on anyone, or let the kids have any more than spending money. Above all, I imagine him advising his son not to get himself killed trying to become Shah.

When I think of Khomeini's deathbed I envision a more politically motivated scene. A story we read in an elementary school textbook comes to my mind. This was the story of a *dehqan,* an ancient rural landlord, teaching his sons to stand by each other. He asks them each to go out and collect the strongest twig they can find. When they all come back the father asks them to break each twig. The sons are strong young men and can easily do that. Then the old father bundles the twigs together and asks each son to try to break the bunch. No one can. "You stick together and no one can harm you," he advises his sons. "Alone, you will be snapped in two like twigs."

I imagine an Islamic version of this scene, a *bey'at,* taking place at Khomeini's deathbed. I imagine Khomeini advising his most prominent associates that they can engage in faction fighting only up to a point. They should never forget that the survival of each depends on the survival of all.

It is certainly easier to imagine an intimate deathbed scene with the Shah than with Khomeini. After all, on leaving Iran the Shah wept and knelt down to kiss Iranian soil goodbye, whereas when Khomeini was asked what he felt on returning to Iran after fourteen years of exile, he famously replied: "Nothing." And I myself have no personal encounters with Khomeini to draw on. The closest I have come to a glimpse into Khomeini's personal life was what a friend of mine who is related to him told me years ago when Khomeini was still alive. He said that Mrs. Khomeini had confided in my friend's mother that *"agha"* had become so old and absent-minded that "he forgets to close the door when he goes to the bathroom."

The funny thing is that I have a good many friends, all cousins, through whose family the Shah becomes related to Khomeini: One side of the family is related to the Shah and the other to Khomeini. I wouldn't be surprised if there are other such families. It also amuses me that the wife of one of the top leaders of the communist party in Iran was from high Qajar aristocracy. But it shouldn't be a surprise. Elite is elite.

In real life, I often straightened out my father's bed while he napped on the couch. I took peeks into what he was reading in the copystore-bound manuscripts around and under his pillows. Sometimes I would get distracted and stay there reading, trying to imagine things through the eyes of a man whose life was coming to an end. "It's a good thing some of these were never published," my father would say, thwarting my efforts to glimpse into the mind of a dying man. "They're not very good."

Digital reconstruction

Iraj, an old family friend, offered to host a gathering in memory of my father. Though much younger than my parents, he is part of the circle of their friends, the people I know and like best in Iran. We invited only the closest and oldest friends to this memorial. The connections between us feel ancient—friendships that transcend not just personal histories but a greater history that has so far taken three decades of our lives. Most of the older people that night also have a history of working together professionally, on projects and in ways of which the next generations have only dreamed. And they are all very well aware how they have survived by a hair. Watching the lively and youthful group, many of them pushing eighty, I thought that a secret gratification we share is the knowledge that not many people in the world know such supra-historical friendships.

Iraj, brother of one of our most famous painters, is the architect who designed our old house in Tehran. The house had an understated design that left a lingering impression on discerning people, including a young architect I met years later who was a niece of a later owner. (A mutual friend had mentioned my name and she had asked whether I was related to the original owner of that marvelous house.) My parents sold the house a couple of years before the revolution. The second owner was a rich rug merchant from the bazaar who covered the floors with multiple layers of exquisite rugs, the worth of which far exceeded the price of the house. When my father sold him the house, the rug merchant was so kind as to have our (humble) rugs professionally cleaned into the bargain.

For several years after the revolution my mother was barred from leaving the country. She had run schools and welfare programs for the deaf, most of whom were too poor to afford tuition or other services. She received public funding for her schools and programs. The reputation of her schools, which were started by her father, was impeccable and they served as models for both educational and public-service institutions. Immediately after the revolution, accusations against anyone or any institution successful under the previous regime were rampant, and my mother was accused of being a double agent for CIA and KGB and for channeling public funds to the royal family. To defend herself against these accusations she called a public meeting at her school. Expecting many of the children's families to show up, chairs were set up in the schoolyard. The walnut tree planted in the memory of my grandfather stood in one corner of the yard.

Tension was high during the meeting. Revolutionary guards from the local *komiteh* trickled in, planting themselves in the audience and resting the butts of their semi-automatics against the back of chairs. Many of them were no more than neighborhood boys with access to guns and they let slip afterwards that they had instructions not to let my mother speak to the assembly. "You will fall under her spell if you let her speak," they were warned. "She can convince you of anything." To battle against this outcome the crowd became especially vicious, drowning her voice.

At one point the bizarre hostility grew to such an extent that my mother's brother, who had by accident dropped by the school, felt compelled to stand up and speak in her defense. He was quite shocked by what he had stumbled into. He called the walnut tree planted in my grandfather's memory witness to the madness that had created a mob out of the same people who had cried in gratitude when their children were enrolled in the school. He was so angry that the force of his gesture pointing to the tree ripped his watch off his wrist and flung it at the tree. The commotion caused by my uncle's outburst shielded my mother while she was smuggled out through the back door and into hiding. She escaped that day with, if not her life, certainly her freedom.

It was friends of my parents, a couple, who saved her that day and afterwards. The wife, who had been at the school meeting, whisked her off to the safety of her own mother's house. My mother lived in hiding until with the help of this friend's husband, a prominent surgeon, the worst charges against her were dropped. This is an example of the episodes that connect our group of friends.

Even when the worst charges were finally dropped, my mother was still not allowed to leave the country. The rest of our family was in the U.S. and to join us after nearly four years, she had to leave illegally. She was smuggled out of the country through the mountains of Kurdistan into Turkey. Her companions on this trip included others from our extended group of friends, one of whom was a young mother who was kidnapping her own son. Her husband had recently died and according to the new laws the custody of her son had gone to her husband's family. She and her little boy and new husband made it safely to Canada. It took my mother another two years to finally make her way to the U.S., after a stint as a refugee in France.

The hurried sale of the apartment that had been bought with money from our old house financed my mother's escape. She lived alone in this apartment during some of the darkest and bloodiest years after the revolution. At one point during that time, depressed and melancholic, she went to visit our old house. She just rang the bell one day and asked if she might come in to take a look. The owners, whom she had not seen since they bought the house, were kind as usual and welcomed her in, but it was obvious that things were not well. The household was in deep mourning. Two of the family's children, a daughter and a son, had been executed within months of each other. The house was draped in black and my mother left quite sobered up. After changing hands a few more times the house was finally demolished and replaced by a high-rise in black stone.

Justly proud of his work, for a number of years now Iraj has been looking for photographs of that house in its original form (later owners had made changes). The photos that any of us might have had have vanished through years of moves from house to house, country to country, and city to city. I always have those photos in the back of my mind whenever I come across any of my family's old boxes hastily packed sometime and stored somewhere. But Iraj has finally given up. He said that he is just going to digitally reconstruct the house from the design drawings. "We can even animate it," he said.

Interestingly, digital reconstruction was the reason I had gone to Iran. I went to reconnect with my interest in publishing.

Blueprint

K, whose escape through the Pakistan border I wrote about years ago, is my cousin Kaveh who lives in Istanbul. When I wrote about him in 1987 he was a music student. Now he is a college professor in composition and sound technology and performs his own music on the side. In the summers he has lucrative gigs playing at clubs on the Aegean coast, something he started doing as a summer job over twenty years ago.

I rode behind Kaveh on his motorcycle in Istanbul. He is as good as a native Turk now and it was a treat to ride with him through old neighborhoods one can only visit with a local. I accompanied him to his university where he held office hours at the campus café, advising registering students. I saw him through his students' eyes: knowledgeable in classical composition and the latest technology, successful as a composer and performer of pop music, and very hip driving a motorcycle in a tank top. His younger brother, who left Iran as a child, has a union job playing bass with Istanbul Opera and is married and relatively settled down. Kaveh may not lead as conventional a life but he seems quite in his element in Istanbul and his profession.

I was taken by surprise when out of the blue one day he asked me, "Do you know what a blueprint is?" I told him what I thought it meant. "No, no," he said, "not in that sense." He told me that a Dutch guy he had met told him that your blueprint is that which you were put on this world to do. "I have been asking myself why I've done music all my life," he said. Kaveh's parents were both well-known musicians in Iran and when the family moved to Turkey the music world was the most immediately accessible to him. "But I'm not sure what my calling really is," he said. Then he added thoughtfully, "I have to go to Iran to find my blueprint."

I don't know about blueprints but I am familiar with what Milan Kundera calls "lost destiny." Eastern Europeans certainly have experience with being "thrown off their life's path" by the insipid ideology, savage ignorance, and "virulent faith" espoused by their states. Iranians have lived through something similar. We know how the element crucial to setting your destiny in motion can be snatched from under your nose. But I also know that, oddly enough, many exiled Iranians have actively rejected opportunities that promised to set in motion new and, to all appearances, perfectly good destinies for them. Kaveh is an example; I am another.

My uncle (of the flying wristwatch), Kaveh's composer father, once said that of all the unfortunate people in the world we are the most fortunate. Very true. Many Iranian exiles have had the good fortune to embark on new destinies even more successful than their original ones would have been. But I look at my own friends and acquaintances and wonder why so many have so doggedly, it seems, resisted. Why this clinging to the "original" instead of accepting the "new and improved"?

What my cousin's concern over his "blueprint" also reminded me of is that while many of our peers in the west search for their true calling at different stages of their lives, only exiles feel the need to return to a previous life in a different part of the globe to look for theirs. The path we were thrown off lies elsewhere. After all, here I was, having finally found what I really wanted to do, going back to the path that was initiated by my first job in Iran. The drive behind my trip was not the question "Who am I?" but "Where was I...?"

Where I was, where I left off, was selling books on Shahreza Avenue across from Tehran University.

Taqi Jafari

A book I read last spring helped me retrace my steps back to my high school days when I worked in a bookstore. It was the memoir of Abdorrahim "Taqi" Jafari, founder of Amir Kabir publishing house, the biggest in Iran before the revolution. It not only took me back to my interests as a very young person but placed the era of my youth in the greater context of the nearly nine decades of Jafari's life. More importantly, it gave an excellent account of how destinies in Iran have not just been lost but quite literally stolen.

Jafari was born in 1919, a year after the end of World War One. Though we have all heard the stories, it is not easy to imagine Iran during the first world war: British, Russian, and Ottoman troops at large; the last Qajar Shah roaming Europe while the country disintegrated at the hands of local warlords; famine, cholera, typhus; destitute European refugees; bread made of flour cut with sawdust; death and devastation at home and in the news. It was still war time when Jafari's mother, daughter of a poor widow, was married off to a middle-aged shopkeeper who promised some protection. When at thirteen she gave birth to Jafari in Tehran, the father had already abandoned them and vanished in the provinces. Mother and grandmother raised the child on a pittance of an income from spinning thread for a small socks manufacturer. Jafari's earliest memories are of interminable nights watching two weary women bent over the spinning wheel, working until the wick burning in a dish of oil flickered out. With the death of the grandmother the very young mother was left alone to fend for herself and her boy. The child must go to school at any cost. In fifth grade the bright and restless boy dropped out, and the mother had no choice but to find work for him.

The incident that set Jafari on his life's path is a scene worthy of Gogol. During a torrential downpour one night, mother and son return home on a bus. The dirt street is awash in mud. A very young man getting off the bus stumbles onto the mud at their feet, and when Jafari's mother rushes to his help a conversation is struck up. The young man is a worker in a printing house. At the mention of printing house a spark goes off in the young mother's head. *That* is the way to work and study at the same time.

This may have been the moment of conception of Iran's largest publishing house but the arduous labor lay ahead. Jafari started out as an errand boy in a print shop and slowly learned the trade. The work was back-breaking. Workers showed up first thing Saturday morning and lived in the printing house until the following Friday morning, often not seeing the light of day for days. They slept in increments of two hours. Working with lead, many fell sick with tuberculosis. But the young Jafari, often dizzy with sleep, read the pages that the machines spat out. He read books sheet by cut and folded sheet, and page by typeset page. In his rare free time he rented books from other publishers. As his mother had wished, his education continued. Eventually he left to manage the bookstore of a trade publisher, where he met some leading scholars and writers. He felt the great potential of new fields of learning and new books. When he finally set up his own publishing house with the small capital that he had saved from his wages, he had no interest in the common money-making genres: religious tracts, prayer manuals, pictures of saints, calendars showing auspicious and inauspicious days for doing things, and the occasional volume of treatise or classical poetry. The trade publishers of his acquaintance tried to dissuade him. When he persisted, they not just expected but hoped for his failure.

But Jafari's choice of the name Amir Kabir for his publishing house showed that he had ideas beyond earning a living at a trade he had learned. Amir Kabir was the self-made prime minister of Nasereddin Shah Qajar and had been almost single-handedly responsible for building a centralized Iranian state. He was particularly revered for creating modern and secular institutions of higher education. In 1852 Amir Kabir was sent to his death by the Shah as a result of court intrigues. At the bathhouse at Finn Garden in Kashan today, the wax figures of Amir Kabir and the executioner who slashed his veins at that spot depict one of the most tragic moments in modern Iranian history.

Driven by equal measures of intellectual curiosity and enterprising spirit Jafari built his own version of the great Amir Kabir's legacy. He educated the public as he educated himself. He saw the potential of the market for new works and ideas and devoted his considerable energy to building and expanding this market. He helped create a reading public. By giving decent contracts and royalties to his authors and translators, the former print house worker ended up supporting a class of professional intellectuals. As businessmen go he was a rare breed—he took financial risks on the market for intellectual pursuit. And, lo and behold, Amir Kabir grew and prospered.

Jafari's memoir is a monumental work, and not just because it is the memoir of an extraordinary man. It is the history of an era told through the publishing of the books that helped define it. Amir Kabir's 1979 catalogue lists close to 2,000 titles—classic and contemporary Iranian as well as translations—in fiction, science, history, poetry, social science, philosophy, art. The titles include encyclopedias and dictionaries whose commissioning was itself of historical significance. The translations were of works from not only the west but India, China, Africa, Latin America, and Eastern Europe. The children's series, "Tales of Nations," included collections of stories from around the globe, from Vietnam and Cambodia to Sweden and ancient Greece to American Indians. The choice of Amir Kabir's two most opulent volumes was symbolic: the Shahnameh and the Koran, representing ancient Iran and Islam.

Jafari was tireless and insatiable. He turned down no

good title. He labored over every aspect of production. He sought out, negotiated with, and cajoled the best and sometimes most difficult authors, translators, artists, and printers. His wife sat behind the register at the store and helped him proof galleys at night; his children edited and translated. He was active with the Publishers and Booksellers' Guild. He was instrumental in streamlining the production and distribution of high school textbooks. His business conduct and books were unobjectionable. He was a self-made man with no ties to the previous regime, a true son of the working class, and a heartfelt, practicing Muslim.

A few years after the revolution, after a great deal of persecution and then jailing, he emerged from Evin prison with the government in possession of his company and assets.

But Jafari's memoir ends before the darkest years of his persecution. The final paragraph describes his return home after his first detention at Evin and the premature celebration of his family. It ends: "None of us knew of the storm that was gathering and the catastrophes that were to rain on us..." Then follows an editorial comment: "The second part of this memoir will be published soon."

The fate of the second part of the memoir was very much on my mind when I went to see Jafari in Tehran. I had looked forward to this meeting with great anticipation—it was, in a way, the highlight of my trip. Jafari's memoir was a map of the intellectual development of my generation; I wanted to give him my respects. I was also curious to meet the formidable tycoon who later acquired the publishing house at whose bookstore I had worked.

My decision in eleventh grade to work in a bookstore during summer vacation was a novelty. Middle class high school students in Iran did not work summer jobs. I worked two consecutive summers before leaving for college in the U.S. My friendship with one of my oldest friends, Sohrab, dates from that time. On this recent trip I almost had to drag Sohrab to accompany me to visit our old store in the bustling book-row across the street from Tehran University. He kept shaking his head: "It really is not what it used to be. The best bookstores are not there any more." His wife added, "He can't go for so long without smoking." Sohrab is a chain smoker and smoking is prohibited during Ramezan. We picked a time close to *eftar* so he wouldn't have to suffer for long.

"Out of print, college, foreign," yelled the hired hands on the crammed sidewalks of our old haunt. "Come on up, come on up…" Everyone was selling books: in storefront shops, up in the mezzanines of buildings, inside cavernous book malls, on *basat* spreads on the sidewalks. The store windows were packed with a random clutter of obscure titles, obscure publishers, obscure authors and translators with "Dr." titles. "How to" books, domestic and imported mysticism, software manuals, modern poetry, religious tracts, reprints of old favorites (quite possibly without authors' consent or contract), good books, bad books, printed matter that could hardly be called books… It was like a Google search come to life.

Our old bookstore, the flagship store of Jibi Books Corporation, was at the time the largest bookstore in the country. It was new and shiny and spacious. Every new book passed through many caressing hands before being placed on the shelves: the publisher, distributor, book seller, random employee, random customer… Hot discussions ensued on whether or where the new title should be displayed. It was lots of fun. Now we had a hard time finding the old store. We finally identified it by its familiar shelves; otherwise it was indistinguishable from the other crammed and noisy stores. Where we used to have sitting chairs grouped together for impromptu chats were now racks and racks of books. The store itself was cut in half. The west wing had been turned into storage where a few scruffy, distributor types were unpacking boxes.

"You're from the days before Jafari?" asked one of them, looking me up and down. "Boy, you are old…!" I guess it showed on my face that I thought he was a scruffy, distributor type.

The fate of this bookstore is an interesting one. Jibi Books was owned by the Iranian office of Franklin Book Program. The Iranian "Franklin" (as it was called) was established in the 1960s by its American parent organization to promote books by American authors and give technical and financial assistance to Iranian publishers. But under its first Iranian director it became increasingly independent from the American organization. Eventually, Tehran Franklin became so successful and profitable that it lent financial support to its nonprofit parent in New York. But it accomplished a great deal more. It played a significant role in standardizing, printing, and distributing school textbooks. It collaborated with many publishers (including Jafari) in commissioning and producing new titles. Its imprint, Jibi Books, was an effort to make books more accessible by producing many titles in *jibi* (pocket) editions and selling at more affordable prices. ("There must be a line of books priced at the cost of a sandwich," the director believed.) This and other projects continuously expanded. The editorial board of the organization had an excellent reputation.

By the mid-1970s, however, the second director of Tehran Franklin pulled off a spectacular coup of corruption. He cashed in most of the corporation's considerable assets and settled with the pocketed money in Los Angeles. When he auctioned off Jibi Books and its three bookstores, Jafari bought it. Two years later the revolution came along and what was left of Tehran Franklin was confiscated and renamed "Center for the Promotion of the Islamic Republic." When the zealous new director of Tehran Franklin called Jafari to discuss the purchase of Jibi, the conversation took place across a desk with an unsheathed gun placed on it. "You must return Jibi," Jafari was told. The agreement was reached that Amir Kabir would be reimbursed and Jibi would be returned to the new Franklin. A few months later Jafari was informed that the money was ready and that his employees were to hand over the bookstores on a certain date. On that day Jafari went to our old flagship store, waiting to conduct the transaction. Instead, he received a phone call that the reimbursement had after all not been approved. Jafari writes that during that phone call the name of a certain official in the Revolutionary Council was mentioned, the significance of which did not quite register with him. It did not occur to him that there were now ways in which not just Jibi but the entire Amir Kabir operation could be had for nothing. It was now natural that the reimbursement budget was not approved.

When I finally met Jafari, he was every bit as formidable at 88 as he had ever been. As we chatted in his living room his children one by one joined us. We talked about print-on-demand technology, electronic publishing, the internet, book returns, distribution, paper weight. We had much to say and not a lot of time. We talked about the translation of his memoir, the difference between Iranian and non-Iranian readership. But the second part of the memoir...? I was burning with curiosity.

A heavily self-edited version has been stalled in the Ministry of Guidance for some time now. There is no telling when we will be able to read Jafari's account of his years after the revolution. This much, however, we can surmise: The history of this era will not be told in the books he has published. It will have to be told through accounts of deceit, betrayal, persecution, plunder, prison, and other horrors that have so far remained unspoken. And the publication of the unedited version of the memoir—the un-self-censored version, that is—will have to be referred to our old friend, that unique realm of possibilities: *Inshallah...*

Dr. Khanlari

I never did cross Shahreza Avenue to become a student at Tehran University. I left the country to go to college and ended up graduating from a much more acclaimed American university. But it was the literature department of Tehran University that set both intellectual and personal standards for me. Those standards were particularly well exemplified in the person of Parviz Natel Khanlari, one of Tehran University's most celebrated professors.

The last time I saw Dr. Khanlari was in 1987 when he told me that studying literature belonged to another time. "It is a different world now," he said. I was a graduate student then and his advice to me was to start on a different path while I was still young.

Khanlari was a great man—so great, in fact, that a mere listing of his accomplishments does him no justice. People still argue whether his most important contribution was his journal *Sokhan* (unparalleled to this day in the talent and rigor it fostered), his country-wide literacy projects (leading to a considerable hike in literacy rates), his role in standardizing and producing text books (the accessibility and quality of which we all took for granted), his various cultural organizations (reclaiming, as it were, "Iranian Studies" for our own scholars), the breadth and depth of his research (his definitive studies in Persian language, literature, and intellectual history), or his mark on contemporary writing (the clarity of his prose and brilliance of his poetry are aspired to by the best). The true measure of his greatness is that his influence reached from a broad, grass-roots level all the way up to the heights of cultural production.

Khanlari was also a successful man. Perhaps the most eye-catching part of his curriculum vitae was that he served as deputy minister of interior, minister of education, and senator under the Shah. It was this aspect of his career that helped him accomplish as much as he did and brought severe punishment upon him after the revolution.

The story of how Khanlari "fell in the trap of politics," as both his supporters and detractors put it, is interesting. In the late 1940s he wrote a series of articles in *Sokhan* that became famous as the "bread and literacy" articles. He was troubled over the country's high illiteracy rate and argued that for a developing nation literacy is as crucial as bread. When he accepted his first government post as deputy interior minister, he was widely criticized by the intelligentsia. This was shortly after the coup in 1953 that ousted the hugely popular Mosaddeq and reinstated the Shah. Khanlari was seen as lending legitimacy to the irreparably compromised new regime. In an open letter he published in *Sokhan*, "To My Young Friends," he explained that he took the appointment as the opportunity to put his words into action. "I am a teacher," he wrote. "I consider teaching the most honorable of all professions and I will be a teacher as long as I live."

By the time he was appointed minister of education a few years later, he had become the most vocal critic of the ministry. The various literacy campaigns of the previous decades (mostly the *akaber* programs in urban areas) had been ineffective in design and riddled with poor management. Khanlari was convinced that literacy campaigns must reach the rural population and espoused the excellent idea of creating a "knowledge corps" *(Sepah-e Danesh)* that would use educated army conscripts to serve as teachers—not just of reading and writing, but also of health and other development matters—in villages throughout the country.

There is an interesting anecdote of a meeting where Khanlari was summoned to present and defend his knowledge corps before the Shah and a number of generals. In a typical more-catholic-than-the-pope posture (or as we say in Persian, "bowl hotter than the soup") several of the generals tried to convince the Shah that the project was detrimental to the very foundation of monarchy. A literate population does not make a submissive nation, they advised him. Khanlari pointed out that any number of monarchies in Europe had survived the high literacy rates of their people. He also argued that teaching Persian to all Iranians, whether they were native Persian speakers or not, would have a unifying effect on the country. To the Shah's credit, he was not dissuaded by his generals. Khanlari's knowledge corps was established and eventually branched out into three distinct corps in literacy, health, and development education *(Sepah-e Danesh, Behdasht,* and *Tarvij va Abadani)*. But over the years, like a great many other good ideas, the knowledge corps suffered from the executive bad faith and corruption that derailed and ruined many other intelligent and sincere efforts. Khanlari himself did not last long in his post as minister of education.

As historical irony would have it the generals were not entirely wrong. By the end of the Shah's reign, over 160,000 male and 33,000 female members of the literacy corps had managed to make a significant educational impact on the population. What they had to teach, both in skills and ideas, however, was not compatible with political oppression and gross economic disparity. In fact, exposure to the harsh living conditions of rural Iranians radicalized the corps and, along with them, the people they taught.

Leaving the ministry of education, Khanlari went back to research and higher education, founding the Foundation for Iranian Culture *(Bonyad-e Farhang-e Iran)*. Broad as both the reach and appeal of his literacy programs were, this project plumbed the depths of Iranian culture. For one thing, it was a systematic and rigorous effort to rescue the study of Iranian intellectual history from Orientalist scholarship. The Foundation began by publishing manuscripts of centuries-old Iranian scholarship in all fields: literature, history, art, science, social science. It established research groups that studied and edited old and forgotten manuscripts. Eventually a graduate academy affiliated with the foundation *(Pazhouheshkadeh-ye Farhang-e Iran)* was created for which Khanlari handpicked candidates from his graduate students at Tehran University, giving them practical training in research, editing, and publishing. He developed relationships with Kabul University, trained a number of Afghan students, and established a chair for the teaching of Poshtu at Tehran University. He even introduced programs to revive the teaching of Persian in India and Pakistan, an old tradition that was vanishing in those countries.

When the revolution came Khanlari and his foundation were in peak performance. Within months of the official victory of the revolution, Khanlari was jailed. If any one had a working relationship with the previous regime he did. There was no need to unearth evidence—his work had been entirely public. His arrest was terrifying for all those who knew him. This was a time when people were executed daily on the whims of unknown individuals. Four months in prison took a toll on Khanlari's health. The brutality he endured during his incarceration drastically worsened the early stages of Parkinson's disease. For years after his release, he continued to be subjected to periodic interrogations and harassment. His assets—a house and a collection of books—were finally released a decade later.

It is said that Khanlari's life was spared at the intervention of Ayatollah Motahhari, one of the original leaders of the Islamic revolution, who himself was gunned down shortly afterwards. It is certainly true that even in the heat of revolutionary hatred it was not possible to altogether deny the value of Khanlari's services to the country or denigrate his name. His daughter tells of an interrogation session where at the appearance of Khanlari a revolutionary guard broke into the recitation of his most famous poem, "The Eagle." Khanlari himself told me in 1987 of another interesting encounter with revolutionary guards. At one point armed guards were assigned to his house to keep an eye on him while he silently worked behind his desk. Eventually, I imagine bored with watching a man read and write for hours at a stretch, the guards started noticing the books. Before they knew it, Khanlari had them sitting down and reading with him. (I wish some of us had been so lucky.)

At Khanlari's release from jail, Mehdi Akhavan Sales, one of our best contemporary poets, wrote a poem of consolation to him after a famous ghazal of Hafez, *Chenan namand-o chenin niz nakhahad mand* ("Such as it was it is no more and this too will not remain"). "You have left behind great works that do honor to the world of literature, may you persevere and continue," he said. "The great menace of this season of winter will pass / The turn for another spring will come."

Not one to miss the chance to reply in poetry, Khanlari wrote back a ghazal in the same pattern. "There is indeed hope for spring after the worst winter," he acknowledged. "But what use... Hope and joy do not return to one in old age." In reply to Akhavan's hope that he would continue to "honor" the literary world with his works, he wrote: "Every honor I earned became a burden to me, why do I need to add to it?" His last line is the most poignant: "May you live happily, my friend of joyful times / For on my heart spring itself has placed yet another burden."

When this paragon of learning told me to abandon my studies I did not take him seriously. I was aware of what had happened to him but I also knew that he knew better than anyone that ignorance and brutality have never managed to diminish the worth or attraction of literature. I'm almost sure he didn't even expect me to take his advice—more likely, he was testing me in a version of his screening of graduate students. (He insisted on maintaining a low budget for his organization because he said he wished to discourage any motivation other than "love.")

Khanlari's dignity and kindness were his trademarks. He never lost them even under the most extreme conditions. His composure and his respect for the intelligence of even his tormentors were disarming. Even at the height of his success he was not authoritarian or driven by vanity. But deep inside his eyes sparkled an exacting wit whose cutting edge he did not often reveal. His sense of humor was exquisitely wicked. (He was Sadeq Hedayat's close friend, after all.) I remember even as a child trembling a little in his presence, feeling that he could see right through me. Later, I could see that in spite of his gentle and soft-spoken manner, his eye for inauthenticity, vulgarity, and corruptibility was flawless. To this day I remain insecure as to whether I was of the caliber to be one of his chosen graduate students. At any rate, despite his advice to the contrary I did not abandon my intellectual pursuits. But I did understand how "spring" weighed on him like a burden. I could see for myself that "this is a different time now." When I returned to the U.S. I asked my dissertation advisor whether he thought continuing my studies was worth the effort. "I don't know," was all he said. By the time I finished my degree my expectations had sunk so low that there was no point in pursuing an academic career. Khanlari's advice worked its effect on me gradually.

Before my recent trip to Iran I randomly snatched a book from a recycling pile, Evelyn Waugh's *Vile Bodies*. At some point, one of the characters, a Father Rothschild, compares his generation to the "bright young things" of England in the 1920s. "My private schoolmaster used to say, 'If a thing's worth doing at all, it's worth doing well,'" he says. "But these young people have got hold of another end of the stick, and for all we know it may be the right one. They say, 'If a thing's not worth doing well, it's not worth doing at all.' It makes everything very difficult for them."

I too, after all, belonged to His Majesty's spoiled-brat generation. I wanted the best of all possible worlds. If I couldn't work with someone like Khanlari I wouldn't work with anyone at all. (And Waugh's Father Rothschild was right, it did not make things any easier for me!)

Khanlari died in 1991. Luckily for us, he did not abandon work during his home-bound years. The Hafez he edited during this time set a daunting standard of scholarship and taste—it remains to be seen whether it can be emulated any time soon. Two months after his death, his wife and colleague Zahra Kia Khanlari died. Zahra Khanom, as she was known, was his classmate from graduate school and among the first women to graduate with PhDs from Tehran University. The school children of my generation were introduced to the Persian literary canon through her incorporation of the classics into our elementary textbooks.

Their daughter Taraneh told me that during his last days in the hospital her father often appeared to be conversing with the great masters he had spent his life reading and studying. At some point a visitor put an absurd question to him: "How old are you, Dr. Khanlari?" He smiled through his closed eyes. "Two thousand five hundred years old," he said. It was a quintessential Khanlari reply: part inside joke, part absolute truth.

I believe Khanlari was the only man who had an answer worthy of Montesquieu to his famous question: "How can one be Persian?"

Yesterday

A relatively obscure little book came out last summer with the unusual title ... *to Today*. It is a history of Iran's largest commercial print house, Offset Corporation, in the words of its four executive directors from 1957 to now. The book was published more as a commemoration (50th anniversary of the company) than to attract a wide readership. The title of the book is especially noteworthy. The story of "Offset" (as the company is called) makes an interesting random example of the yesterday that is omitted from the title.

The history of Offset also goes back to Franklin Book Program. Homayoun Sanatizadeh, the first director of Tehran Franklin, was picked by the American nonprofit to open a Tehran branch because, as he himself put it, he knew nothing about publishing. Old trade publishers and printers in Iran were set in their ways and resisted the overhauling of the industry that new western technology had made inevitable. To publish the books that Tehran Franklin had in mind, new technology was indispensable. Sanatizadeh was encouraged by New York Franklin to open a printing house using the latest offset technology. The main obstacle was technical know-how and trained personnel.

Offset Corporation was established in 1957 with capital loaned to it from Tehran Franklin and with Seyyed Hasan Taqizadeh as Chairman of the Board. (Taqizadeh was a seasoned diplomat and one of the leading figures of the 1905 constitutional revolution.) The work force was supplied by the orphanage that Sanatizadeh's family ran in Kerman. Young people with no family and few prospects were just the right group to withstand the grueling working conditions of a print shop. They were also bright and ready to learn a trade. But, lest you imagine some Dickensian scenario, these workers were better paid (with overtime for the after-hours that printers customarily worked) and taken care of (with a housing subsidy, for example) than workers elsewhere. And lest you suspect that the Americans set up Offset to sell their obsolete machinery to Iran, Sanatizadeh bought state-of-the-art equipment from Germany.

While Sanatizadeh was working to set up Offset, a sad but inevitable rift occurred between a father, the owner of Taban printing house, and his son Amir Samimi. The young Samimi was sent by his father to England and Germany to study the latest in printing technology but when he returned to Iran he encountered resistance to the very technology that he had been sent to Europe to learn. Samimi's father, like other letterpress printers of the day, considered the new offset technology an unnecessary expense. Samimi left his father's establishment in search of work that would employ his new skills. Sanatizadeh, who was a Taban client, encouraged Samimi to submit a resumé at Franklin. This resumé made its way to New York and convinced the Americans that Tehran Franklin had the qualified personnel to run a modern printing house. Feeling torn by working for a print shop that would be competing with businesses like his own father's, Samimi refused the post of executive director of Offset. He signed on as technical and production director.

Samimi was a proud and confident young man. While negotiating for a salary with Sanatizadeh he refused to name a figure. "You and I don't know each other," he said. "Let us work together for two months and then you pay me whatever you think I'm worth. If I see that you have evaluated me correctly, I'll stay." At the end of two months he did stay, and in 1960 he became executive director after all.

Offset took off. Management was sound and personnel stellar. The quantity of production once and for all ended the textbook shortages that students met with every year. And the quality of the work was unprecedented—so unprecedented, in fact, that the Shah had to investigate in person to believe it. That is an interesting story.

The Royal Library was in possession of an illuminated manuscript of the Shahnameh known as the "Baysonghori" edition. It is a 15th century work with magnificent miniatures. The court planned to give reproductions of this manuscript as gifts to the dignitaries visiting Iran for the 1971 celebrations of the anniversary of 2500 years of monarchy. Samimi heard that a print house in Switzerland was being considered for the work at the cost of 5 million Swiss francs. He went to see the director of the Royal Library to suggest that Offset print the book in Iran—it certainly would make a more meaningful gift than something produced in Switzerland. "It's impossible to reproduce such a work in Iran," the director brushed him off angrily. "This manuscript is so valuable that we can't even take it out of the safe. We cannot take any such risks with it"— implying that Iranian technicians could not be trusted with such delicate jobs. Samimi did not give up. He managed to pull enough strings to get the permission to reproduce one sample page. Offset insured the manuscript for millions of dollars and bought a special safe for it. At length a designated page was photographed and the sample was produced and sent to court.

A period of silence followed while Samimi nervously awaited a response. One day at work he unexpectedly heard the crackling of the gravel driveway as a car pulled up. The driver of the convertible walked out and headed straight for the print shop. It was the Shah. He had come to see for himself that the reproduced page was indeed an Iranian job (he had been falsely informed that through the Franklin connection it was Americans who had done the work). "Who has printed this page?" he asked. "The people you see here," replied Samimi. Apparently the work produced in Iran had surpassed the quality of the sample page done by the Swiss company with whom the director of the Royal Library was anxious to make a deal. After the visit from the Shah, Offset got the job and the director of the Royal Library was dismissed. "We would have done it for free because it was such good publicity for us," said Samimi. But the court did pay for the printing (at a fraction of the Swiss price) and it supplied the paper and ink.

While the reproduction of the Baysonghori Shahnameh was in the works at Offset, Jafari of Amir Kabir was also at work on producing a new Shahnameh. His version was being adorned by contemporary painters, calligraphers, and illuminators. This edition was also expertly printed at Offset. The master copy with all the original art was a proud possession of Amir Kabir, which luckily Jafari donated to the Ferdowsi Museum in Tous two years before the revolution, or it would have also disappeared with the rest of Amir Kabir's confiscated archives. The manuscript is still displayed, without acknowledgement of the donor, at the museum.

In the 1970s Offset became a formidable presence in the Iranian publishing industry. It moved to a large and newly built compound on the outskirts of Tehran in Sorkheh Hesar. It was a very successful company, reflecting the confidence and independence of its executive director. Samimi followed the diligence of the founders in accounting practices. Taqizadeh had made a strong case for paying taxes properly: "If you take 50 tomans from me you have robbed one person, but if you cheat the government of even one rial of tax you have robbed the nation." Offset also set an example in its labor policies. It had a co-op store and a credit union for its workers. It provided free lunches and transportation for the commute from the city. But the workers continued to work long hours and the pay was not what it might have been. Samimi tried to raise the wages but was curtailed by the ministry of labor. "They said increasing wages at one company creates an imbalance in pay scales everywhere and leads to trouble for the government," Samimi says in the book. Unable to raise wages, Samimi decided to compensate his workers in a different way. He provided good health and disability insurance and an adequate retirement pension. Good benefits, management, and working conditions made Offset a desirable place to work. So in 1979 when the revolution triumphed, Offset was expected to withstand any investigation into its finances and affairs.

The day that Jafari was called to Franklin to discuss the fate of Jibi Books across the desk with a loaded gun placed on it, his conversation with the new director was interrupted by a telephone call. It was Samimi's wife enquiring about the arrest of her husband. Samimi had been summoned by this director a few days earlier and without a word of discussion was arrested by revolutionary guards. Despite the profusion of weapons on display in the office that day, no one seemed to have handcuffs. After a scramble to find something that would do the job, Samimi's hands were tied behind his back with a piece of rope and he was taken directly to Evin. After six months he was released and eventually left for England. (He has never returned.) The new director of Franklin who had him arrested was appointed director of Offset as well and held that position for close to two years.

At my father's memorial gathering the editor of his last two books came with copies of his novel, fresh off the press. It was unfortunate that my father did not live to see his novel printed, but the publishing world in Iran being plagued with all kinds of ills (not all of them the government's fault), it is sweet to lay hands on any new book. It was thanks to the efforts of this friend and editor (a journalist turned historian) that the book had seen the light of publication. I was quite surprised, however, to see that the title had been changed. The original title, *Dirouz* (Yesterday), had been changed to *Bazi-ye Taqdir* (Play of Fate). The publisher had decided that the second title would sell more books.

Dirouz is the story of three friends, an intellectual, a musician, and a socialist activist. All three of them are idealists driven toward unabashedly lofty ideas of truth, perfection, and justice. But what the characters think and how their fates play out is secondary to the light that the title *Yesterday* throws on them. The novel is a reminder of a kind of idealism that belonged to a bygone era. It is an echo of Khanlari's view that "this is a different time." I can hardly be a judge of the marketability of the novel's new title but I know that the change of title missed the point of the book. What was most curious to me, however, was that the word "yesterday" was missing from the covers of two books published last summer. Chances are good that the omissions were coincidental and the reasons quite different. But in a country that has gone through a cultural revolution, the word "yesterday" carries more than the usual connotations. It is not born of nostalgia; it carries historical weight.

This yesterday that keeps popping up is not a reference to the previous regime. It is the yesterday of the "reawakening" of an ancient country (as in *Tarikh-e Bidari-ye Iranian*), the birth of new visions, and the updating of an old consciousness. It is a reference to something that led to the 1905 Constitutional Revolution and continued despite all the setbacks since. It is the yesterday of the struggle for the rule of secular law, equal rights, nationalization of natural resources, and development in the best sense. This yesterday encompasses the brilliance and hard work of generations—indeed, their idealism. It is the sum total of what they built. It stands like the encased and unacknowledged Amir Kabir Shahnameh at the Tous Museum.

A few years ago Jafari visited the Tous Museum, admiring the work he had conceived, financed, and seen to completion through a great deal of trouble. He hung about listening to other visitors' comments. The plaque on the display case cryptically identifies the book as "Shahnameh of Amir Kabir." Most people pass by without giving it a second thought but Jafari heard one man comment sarcastically to his family, "The late Amir Kabir sure went through a lot of trouble for this." The yesterday I'm speaking of is the time from the slashing of the wrists of the great Amir Kabir to the point when a notable piece of work, such as the Shahnameh produced by the publishing house bearing his name, is placed in a glass case in a museum. It is all that was accomplished during this time and which, again like the edition of the Shahnameh coupled with his name, lacks public acknowledgement.

I could have titled this chapter "A tale of the two Shahnamehs"—or *three* Shahnamehs for that matter, the third being the 10th century composition itself. The story of this book is no less an epic and tragedy than the ancient ones it has preserved. In fact, the history of this text, both its creation and its various productions and reproductions, makes an illuminating narrative thread running through a long yesterday of a good thousand years. A great deal of Iranian history is contained in the history of this book.

Ferdowsi labored over the Shahnameh for thirty years. What he accomplished is monumental in the grandest sense.

> *Suffer as I did in these thirty years*
> *I brought Ajam back to life with this Parsi*

Ajam is the word Arabs used for "Iranian" and *Parsi* is the old version of Farsi, the Persian language. True to his own assessment, Ferdowsi is credited with reviving Persian language and culture after Iran's encounter with the formidable Islamic empire. But during the years of the composition of the Shahnameh, Ferdowsi lived in isolation and hardship. He was accused of heresy and the praise of forbidden heroes and kings, and dismissed as a chronicler of forgotten times. He died in poverty, having lost hope of reward from Sultan Mahmoud Ghaznavi to whom he had dedicated his book. But the great poet knew the true worth of his work.

> *I have raised a high palace of verse*
>   *that will not be harmed by wind or rain.*
> *I shall not die for I have lived*
>   *to sow the seeds of sokhan.*

Sokhan is often translated as "discourse" but it could simply mean "word"—a loaded word indeed. Khanlari took the name Sokhan for his monumental journal after this line of the Shahnameh.

Over the centuries the Shahnameh has come to be viewed as the unshakable pillar of Iranian national identity. Legend has it that as Ferdowsi's body was being carried out of one of the gates of Tous for burial, the king's rewards finally reached the town from another gate. (Legend also has it that the daughter for whose dowry Ferdowsi had wanted the reward returned it untouched to Sultan Mahmoud.)

The more things change…

I resort to ellipsis to avoid redundancy, or maybe out of exasperation at having a certain historical phenomenon rubbed in my face. Maybe "yesterday" was omitted from the title of those two books last summer for the same reason. Despite some mighty efforts to eradicate it, yesterday is possibly all too present in people's minds.

Touran Khanom

The yesterday to which I belong was shaped by a generation of exceptional individuals, and it was my extraordinary good luck to have personally known many of them. Over the years my search for others of that caliber has proved not just disappointing but disorienting. And I have found that I am not alone in the need to go back to the source.

In the vicinity of Baharestan, the old Parliament, there used to be an elementary school that was a little gem of an establishment. *Dabestan-e Farhad* opened in 1958 in the building and grounds that had been home to Mirhadi family. Touran Mirhadi—or, as she is universally known, Touran Khanom—was the youngest daughter of the family and the principal of the school. Her old students, some now well into their fifties, still refer to themselves as Farhadi, and are perpetually in quest of establishing contact with each other and their old teachers. For those us living outside Iran, no trip to Tehran is complete without touching base with Touran Khanom.

Touran Mirhadi turned eighty this year—but don't for a minute picture her as a retired educator living with fond old memories, happy to receive the kindness and gratitude of her students. She works round the clock managing major projects, is as sharp and unflappable as ever, and graciously fits seeing us into her very busy schedule. Whenever I see her, alone or in company of other Farhadis, I am struck with one thing: Touran Khanom doesn't need us, we need her. Still.

I made an appointment to see her at the offices of the Children's Book Council *(Shora-ye Ketab-e Koudak)*, one of the oldest and most distinguished NGOs in Iran. CBC has been active since 1962 producing books and initiating all kinds of projects for promoting a lively and literate children's culture in Iran. My favorite part of the "Shora" (as the organization and the office is referred to) is the bulletin board. The variety of projects, events, programs, invitations, auditions, and other activities that are posted on it is impressive. My mother says someone ought to make a photo album of this bulletin board; it would be such a good guide to children's culture in Tehran. Touran Khanom is one of the founding members of the Shora, and her largest project, the Encyclopedia for Young People, is a publication of this organization. Volumes 11 though 14 of the encyclopedia are currently being worked on. Touran Khanom is full of ideas and talk about her work.

The day I visited her at the Shora two other old Farhad students were there, all of us on brief visits from the U.S. These two guys had not been my classmates but I had flickering and dusty recollections of both as little boys, gray goatees notwithstanding. As we sat around a conference table listening to Touran Khanom's challenges and tribulations editing a major encyclopedia, I could not help making a bet with myself that the encyclopedia, monumental as the project is, was not the reason for us being there. I sat there listening to our old principal, conscious of the ticking away of the short time we had with her, asking myself, What is it we want of her?

One of the first things I, for one, have always wanted of her is guidance on how to raise my son. I hang on her every word—even when I disagree with her I don't flatter myself by disregarding her way of doing things. Having been involved with my son's schools in the U.S., I am especially interested in her experience running a school where discipline and freedom coexisted so successfully. I try to discern tips in her conversation. But, in her presence, it is not easy to divert Touran Khanom's attention from what is on her mind. On this day she talked a little about the absurdity of teaching according to children's "developmental stages." She considers most current practices in schools as applications of behavior modification techniques. She abhors any approach that leads to conformity and a herd mentality. "I am convinced that you have to look at and teach each child individually," she says. But how do you practice this principle in running a school and in so many classrooms? "I have written about my own experience in the books about Farhad." She politely declines making nutshell statements. She does not offer a theory. She has no magic formulas, no short-cut "strategies" to impart to eager listeners in one afternoon. Real pedagogy is far too subtle for that. She did not teach down to us when we were kids and she does not pontificate for us now. She listens to our concerns, asks questions, but offers no advice. In typical Touran Khanom fashion, she refers the solution back to us.

Having solutions referred back to us is something we well remember from our days at Farhad. In fact, a lot of things were referred back to us—maintaining order, for instance. Each classroom elected three "representatives" *(namayandeh)* each month who were responsible for a variety of things, from keeping the classroom tidy and airing it during recess, to giving the teacher a hand and aiding communication between teacher and students. Once a week each classroom was on duty on the playground, making sure the little kids were not trampled by rambunctious older ones and resolving disputes and conflicts. "The kids know best how to resolve things between themselves," Touran Khanom always said. At the beginning of the year, along with a new lunch box and uniform, our mothers made us little white armbands with "Namayandeh" embroidered in red thread on it. Learning to be good representatives was simply part of our education. (I can't help but to compare practicing to become a good *representative* to what is now preposterously called *leadership* training for children.)

One of the Farhadis visiting that day remembered an incident in third grade when he was namayandeh during lunch break. A bunch of younger kids had devised a game of *kharbazi*, where they took turns riding each other like donkeys. The game was getting rowdier and more fun by the minute. Torn between his responsibility as namayandeh and the lure of the game, he finally gave in to temptation. He took off his armband, neatly folded and put it in his pocket, and joined the fun. He knew that he would be accountable later to Mohsen Khan (Touran Khanom's husband and second in command) and suffer the consequences—and that was exactly the point: Taking responsibility for our choices is what Farhad School tried to teach.

As I listened to the reminiscences I was busily taking mental notes on discipline tips that I could adapt to present day schools—I have never known more seasoned authorities on the subject than Farhad staff. And yet even that was not what was foremost on my mind. I had recently read Touran Khanom's biography of her mother and certain urgent thoughts had been awakened in me.

I have known Touran Khanom all my life. My mother is a friend and colleague of hers and we are related through her second marriage. The more you know about her life, the more you are humbled by the strength of her character and principles. But I had little idea of the origins of this strength. Reading Touran Khanom's book about her mother opened my eyes to a side of her life I had known very little about. It took me quite by surprise to trace so many of the most profound influences in my life to a woman I had never known.

Touran Khanom's German mother, Greta Dietrich, married Fazlollah Mirhadi and left Europe for Iran with him in 1919. They had met during World War One at a farm where they had taken work in exchange for food and a place to sleep. Mirhadi had left Iran to study in Germany in 1909, fresh from his participation in the Constitutional Revolution of 1905 and full of idealism and hope for the future. The young German woman, disappointed by what she called the "superficiality and sensationalism" of European youth, had been attracted by the "serious, thoughtful, and well-mannered" Iranian revolutionary. She herself had rejected her strict Catholic upbringing, rebelling against what she saw as the conformity and passivity it fostered. She recounted for her children an incident that left a major impression on her. After winning a medal for swimming across a river she received a slap in the face from her father for taking such risk. When she married her Muslim Iranian husband her family was mortified. "At least you could have married a protestant," they said. But even they were eventually impressed by the idealism and hard work of the new son-in-law. At any rate, for Greta Iran was an adventure and an opportunity not just to live a bold and free life herself but to help build a whole new society, starting with her children and their friends. A sculptor by training, she told her five children that she gave up making sculptures "to make you."

She decided that her children would grow up Iranian but also study Europe. During the school year they went to Iranian schools and in the summers she taught them German. She supplemented her children's Iranian education with other subjects: French, English, western music, art, literature. Her passion for building and gardening (she designed their family houses and landscaped the gardens, including the building that later became Farhad School) created the environments for her children's physical and intellectual growth. A strong athlete herself, she made sure that any kid who came her way learned many sports. (My father remembered Touran as a young girl diving off the championship board at Manzariyeh swimming pool.) And through it all she taught the children to think about what they were learning. She listened, she asked questions, and she taught them to ask questions. Greta Dietrich's education of her five children and their numerous friends, combining what she found best in two cultures, was the backbone of the education we received at Farhad.

The title of Touran Khanom's first chapter describing her mother's life in Iran is "Struggle Against Death." Infant and child mortality was very high in Iran in the early twentieth century. Living with a sister-in-law out of whose thirteen children only five had survived, Greta's first struggle was to keep her children alive. "I vowed that none of my children would die," she said.

But the shadow of death and the destruction of two world wars were never far from the Mirhadi family. The First World

War had claimed the lives of eighteen young men in the Dietrich family. It was the devastation of that war that had brought the young German woman and her Iranian husband together. And though by the time of the Second World War the Mirhadi family was far from Europe, the war came to them.

When the Allied Forces occupied Iran in 1941 (the British in the South and the Russians in the north) Touran's father was imprisoned for thirteen months. The Allies banished the Germans working in Iran to Australia and sent most Iranians with personal or professional connections to Germans to internment camps. Mr. Mirhadi, a civil engineer, had worked with the Germans building the main railroad in Iran—the same railroad that was used by the Americans to provide Russian troops with supplies to defeat the Germans in Stalingrad, the single-track railroad that miraculously sustained mammoth American shipments. Greta rented out the Mirhadi house (later Farhad School) to support the family while her husband was in prison.

Touran's older sister who was studying in Germany during the war never quite recovered from the trauma of her experiences, including the loss of her first child. When the war was over she and her Austrian artist husband, released from POW camps in Russia, moved to Hamedan, then a remote little ancient town. She drowned herself in her work as a physician while her husband sank into addiction, neglecting their children by Greta's standards. Unable to bear it, the grandmother ended up adopting her five grandchildren and raising a second set of children. She never came to terms with the effects of the war on her daughter and son-in-law but when she visited Germany after the war she too did not recover from the shock. She said that she didn't recognize her own people anymore. "Perhaps I have become too Iranian," she said.

Two years after the end of the war, Touran Khanom's youngest brother, Farhad, was killed in a traffic accident. Touran herself was studying in Paris and on hearing the news she resolved to do something in his memory. "Great sorrow must be turned into great work," was her consolation. It was the beginning of Touran's own struggle against death. Farhad School was born of this struggle.

Farhad Mirhadi's death was the first tragedy that cast a shadow on our school. The second was the execution of Touran Khanom's first husband, Jafar Vakili, a communist major *(sargord)* in the army. Touran was left with their little boy. "Build a new life," her mother advised her a year after Vakili's death. "If you take on the role of a traditional woman you will not raise a good son and you will make nothing of your own life." And so, with support from her mother and second husband, Mohsen Khomarlou, Touran Khanom started Farhad School.

The execution of Sargord Vakili was of course not talked about at Farhad; any perceived affiliation with the communist party was quite dangerous. But the school reflected the idealism of its founders while trying not to attract too much attention to itself. (Many of the children's parents had socialist leanings.) The tuition was modest and sliding scale. There was no heavy-handed, top-down discipline. While Touran Khanom and Mohsen Khan carried great authority, all school staff (teachers, cooks, janitors, gardeners) were treated with equal respect and recognition. Sargord Vakili, a heroic and revered figure, was simply a part of the school's unspoken mythology and the ultimate embodiment of the school's principle of taking responsibility for one's choices. His son was our schoolmate and although he was not treated any differently, a certain mystique was attached to him. It was impossible for the rest of us to wrap our minds around the idea of an executed father. The thought of having your father, guilty of no crime we could understand, murdered was unfathomable. The execution of Sargord Vakili stood before us like a massive black rock that would not fit into the sunny picture of our childhood at Farhad. Yet there it was. And there was Touran Khanom with her kind second husband, her oldest son growing up a regular boy, and eventually her new little children.

When I was in first grade another tragedy came crashing down. On a violently stormy night during a trip to the

Caspian Sea, two cars holding Touran Khanom and many family members fell off a collapsed bridge into a flooded river and were washed to the sea. Four children and an adult died that night. One of the children was Touran and Mohsen's little son Kaveh. The other casualties were my father's cousins and aunt, so I heard full accounts of the horrors of that night. A strong swimmer, Touran Khanom was at some point pulling Kaveh and another little girl to safety when she was hit by a wave of debris from the bridge and lost her grip on them. Mohsen Khan's brother, who blamed himself for arranging the trip, lost three of his children that night and became a virtual recluse afterwards. At school, I remember that Touran Khanom vanished for what seemed like a very long time. I remember people scrambling to maintain the regular functioning of the school. I remember Mohsen Khan dragging himself around with stooped shoulders and very heavy steps. And I remember the hushed school assembly on the day that Touran Khanom returned to us. She stood before us in her tall and composed figure and explained what had happened in her typical open and direct manner. I was electrified then and tremble now at the thought of how brave a mother must be to face a schoolyard full of children, her children's friends, after losing her own child. I remember she mentioned Kaveh but I don't remember what she said. I'm sure she tried to be reassuring. Many teachers and students were crying. What I best remember, however, is Touran Khanom's voice. I can still hear it. It was filled with tears and the will to courage.

A Farhadi friend who read a draft of this chapter emailed me what she remembered of Touran Khanom's speech to the assembly that day. "Children, four of your friends are not here today because some people did not do their work right," she said. "The bridge they built collapsed because it was not strong enough to hold us. I know you are sad. I am sad too. But we must learn from this accident." My friend has almost perfect recollection of that day because Touran Khanom's advice made a defining impression on her: "It is not important what profession you choose in the future, it is important how you do your work. If you become a builder, be a good builder. If you become a doctor, be a good doctor. You must do your work well and honestly."

A couple of years ago Touran Khanom said that in her mind she still speaks to the four boys and men she last lost: Farhad, Jafar, Kaveh, and Mohsen, who died from cancer shortly after the revolution. In the book about her mother she writes that true love is when someone inspires you to be a better person—and from what I gather from the rest of the book, it has everything to do with the struggle against death.

On the day of our visit to the Shora we—the three Farhadis, Touran Khanom, my mother, and another colleague—sat around the conference table as other colleagues dropped in with shoptalk or just greetings. But I was restless. Piaget, the "Botany" entry of the encyclopedia, and that afternoon's performance of a children's ensemble were all well and good but something else had brought us there. I wondered if she sensed the mute urgency of our being there.

I finally took a risk. "The book you wrote about your mother was very eye-opening for me," I said, "but when will you write about yourself?" I know how much Touran Khanom dislikes talking about herself but I had already started. "We want to know how you have felt living and working through all that has happened to you. We want to know how you did it." My fellow Farhadis nodded vigorously and I was emboldened. I told her that during all these years that she has been observing us we have been observing her too and, frankly, she is a more interesting person than any of us. More than that, she mattered to us in a way that all her thousands of students could not matter to her. My old schoolmates joined in as I made my passionate if somewhat incoherent plea for her to tell us about herself. She looked at us, touched and a little embarrassed, but also a bit puzzled. Could she never have suspected that we saw in her more than just someone doing a good job educating us? Struggle against death is something we have all now faced in many ways but very few of us have done a good job at it.

I was even more incoherent when I visited Touran Khanom at her house a few days later. Before lapsing back into Shora business the first day, my mother had suggested that I articulate more clearly what I wanted Touran Khanom to write. But the more I tried to articulate the more I failed. I said that "we" (having the support of two other Farhadis at that point!) wanted to know what we could do now. "Do...?" Touran Khanom said a shade impatiently. "There is always lots of work to do."

In the years since the revolution Touran Khanom lost her husband and also her school. After the revolution, all private schools were bought from their owners by the ministry of education for nominal fees. Many, especially the co-ed ones, were closed down. I believe Touran Khanom was given the option of staying on as principal of a re-engineered Farhad but declined. She gave all her time to the Shora and the encyclopedia, to which her late husband donated his inheritance. The scarf on her head and the long loose clothing that she took up wearing are mere trivialities to her. The way she looks at the new religious culture, I imagine, is the way her mother looked at Iran back in early twentieth century: It is what it is and you do what you have to do. Personal, political, and historical tragedy are just ways of life.

Touran Khanom writes that in their youth she and her siblings and their friends (and later the next generation) had long discussions with their mother about politics. The young people were full of fury and criticism of the way things were in the country, but Greta would have none of that. "Don't compare Iran to Europe," she would say. "Compare what is now with what was before. Your fathers have done a great deal developing this country and instead of criticizing it you must build on that work." She herself rejoiced in the construction of every new road, tunnel, factory, school and hospital in the country and in every activity that promoted life and health and culture. She was right, of course.

Now, I see the seasoned Touran adopting an even more iron-willed version of her mother's views. She is ready to recount for anyone all the good things that have happened in the country since the revolution. And she's right too; it would be inexcusably ignorant to brush off the works of a nation for three decades, especially against such enormous domestic and international odds. And the cats let out of the bag by a revolution are never to be underestimated—mainly, the confidence of a nation in its ability to ultimately spit out what it doesn't want. I understand. I also know that Touran's powers for willing things into reality are quite out of the ordinary. And sometimes, I think, by its sheer strength the willpower obscures reality.

"People come to talk to me about women's rights but they get disappointed in me," she says in her book. "I tell them Iranian women of merit do not suffer from lack of rights. To claim one's rights one must first become worthy of having rights—and in this there is no difference between men and women." Well, yes and no… I have no doubt that Touran Khanom would never think of a divorced woman who does not have a right to the custody of her children after the age of seven as not being "worthy" of that right. I think that in her battle against a death more devastating and all-encompassing than even the personal losses she has suffered, she is pushing the limits of her mother's determination to see the good things. Or maybe I simply resist trading the young Touran I knew for a version of the middle-aged Greta.

At some point during the day at her house I finally managed to ask her a question that had been weighing on me. "All understood is all forgiven…?" I asked. In typical Touran Khanom fashion she took it in silence. But she did smile.

I gave up trying to convince her to write for us. For the rest of our visit I looked at old photographs while she and my mother talked about publishing children's books. When the taxi driver rang the bell for us she accompanied us to the door. We walked through her lush garden with its old trees, blooming rose bushes, and unobtrusive landscaping. Her house, where she lives with her daughter and her family, is probably one of the last of the old villa-style houses in Tehran. As she opened the gate she bent down to pick up one of the many flyers she receives every day from developers offering to buy her house. I looked with hostility at the ugly large towers going up all around her little beautiful oasis. She didn't let me start. "Nothing wrong with building these huge apartment houses... It is a sign of the rise of the Iranian middle class," she said. "That is not a bad thing."

One of the publishers I talked to in Iran is a publisher of books for and about children. His "History of Children's Literature in Iran," seven volumes so far, is a veritable treasure trove. A great admirer of Touran Khanom, he was in the process of organizing an event in early November, to celebrate the "construct of childhood" in the last one hundred years in Iran, and the many educators, authors, and artists who have contributed to it. It would also commemorate the 80th birthday of Touran Mirhadi with a film about her life. A large elaborate event was planned with over one thousand tickets presold. A great deal of organization went into the event, and it was with enormous relief one week before the date that one of the organizers said, "Nothing left to do but order the flowers..." Two days before the event it had to be cancelled. The permit for the gathering was revoked. No explanation.

The day I talked to this publisher we were short of time and full of shoptalk. We hurriedly exchanged ideas about newsfeeds and RSS and he quickly went over the relative merits of different open source content management software for me. We talked about producing manuscripts that will have to wait for publication in the future. No problem; everyone's sitting on unpublished works. There were lots of people dropping in and out of the room where we were talking—graphic artists, web designers, writers, translators. At one point, when we finally had the room to ourselves, he brought his head close to mine and conspiratorially whispered, "You won't believe what I have here..." He tapped a bulging portfolio. "Material," he said, "for a book about Touran Khanom."

We both smiled. And I thought: What do you know, maybe it is we who must write about Touran Mirhadi. It is the common fate of many small and independent publishers that they must themselves write what they want to publish.

The black hole of survival

In his memoir Taqi Jafari uses an image that has stayed with me.

As he tells the story, a few years before the revolution many people sensed the impending crisis. "This crown prince of ours will never make it to the throne," they muttered under their breath. One of Jafari's associates advised him to cash in his assets and emigrate to the U.S. before it was too late. But Jafari would not dream of it. "I have nothing to fear from a change in the regime," he said. "I have served my country and these books are my roots. Who can cut off my roots?" But of course the change was ruinous to him. He describes it as the felling of a tree he had planted. "The tree was axed, the roots were severed, the branches and leaves wilted, and the flowers died." Writing his memoirs he found himself not just recounting his life and work but contemplating the "hole left in the ground by the uprooted tree."

The reference to this hole makes the image of the uprooted tree doubly apt. One can picture the felled tree with its mighty roots and branches a testament to years of nurture and growth, the magnificent living thing whose life has been cut short. But the tree, in its mutilated form, is visible no matter how hard the regime tries to obstruct the view—what begs closer notice is the hole left in the ground by the uprooting. This black hole has swallowed a great deal over the years.

What cultural revolutions try to do is not just kill trees such as Jafari's, as monuments of the old order of things, but bury the past ("yesterday") in the hole that is left behind. The analogy is not mine. After the revolution, the new regime called the publication of books by authors from pre-revolution days "exhumation." It did its best to bury the intelligentsia along with a certain past. Exploring the hole left by the uprooted tree exposes the falsifications that a cultural revolution is based on, but it turns up a great deal more.

This dark hole has swallowed three decades of life so far. Big chunks of the lives of roughly three generations have now vanished into it—from the peak years of the older generation to the childhood of the youngest. I belong to the middle generation whose coming of age coincided with the revolution. Many died in war and by execution. Many were crushed or lost years in prison. Many left Iran. But most of us who survived, inside or outside Iran, found ourselves sliding into the black hole little by little, day by day.

In the chapter on Touran Khanom I wrote that we, her students, have now had our own struggles against death but are not doing as good a job at it. Most of us lack the discipline of a Touran, the drive of a Jafari, or the vision and forbearance of a Khanlari. Our struggle against death has hardly amounted to more than our own daily survival, reeling from blows while trying to make it from one day to the next. So far we have lost three decades of our lives from, let's say, our twenties to fifties. While my generation was thrown off its life's path, the generation after us had not even the luxury of envisioning such a path. Postponed life, aborted plans, decisions never made, despair, loss, waste—this is the stuff floating inside the darkness of the past three decades. Years went by as we strained to see the light at the end of the tunnel. This seemingly endless wait has been part of Iranian life, within or without the country's borders.

Marz, "border," is an interesting Persian word. It means both the outer limits of a space as well as the area enclosed within those limits. *Marz-e por gohar*—a phrase from *Ey Iran*, the country's national anthem by popular consensus—refers to Iran as a country of jewel-strewn *marz*. Iranians refer to themselves as either *doroun-marzi*, within borders, or *boroun-marzi,* outside borders. Studded with gems or not, *marz* becomes little more than an arbitrary designation to those alienated within or displaced outside of borders.

"Exile" does not apply only to Iranians living outside Iran; it is also the condition of being denied history and existence inside the country. Denial, in fact, is the first thrust in digging black holes. Perhaps the twentieth century will go down in history for the range and depth of its denials. The sheer number of its cultural revolutions, which seem more concerned with the denial and eradication of the past than with building the future, would support this claim. Certainly a great deal of the best literature of the twentieth century, from Russia and Eastern Europe to Latin America, grapples with historical denial. Gabriel García Marquez has called it being exiled from memory. The last blow to the last of the Buendía line in *One Hundred Years of Solitude* is the old priest's denial that Colonel Aureliano Buendía fought thirty-two wars and that three thousand workers were gunned down and their bodies thrown into the sea. There is more historical truth in this fiction than there is nonfiction in so much of what we have been fed as history: Denials delivered with straight faces, smug self-assurance, academic credentials, even a barely masked sneer; storybook nonfiction that spells out for us what exists and what never happened, how things come into being from absolute nothing and vanish into it at whim, what was decreed directly from heaven and what ascends straight back there. Perhaps it is much of the official histories of the twentieth century that ought to be called magic realism. At any rate, even if unlike the Buendías the demise of the Iranian people is not recorded in any chronicle, a great deal of the population, inside and outside the country, has been "exiled from memory" just like that doomed family.

Those Iranians who left the country ran away from the conditions of life in Iran. We ran from isolation, lawlessness, underground living, and daily torments. We ran from threat and constriction. To make it short, we ran from something that is the opposite of freedom. Most of us had no intention of becoming immigrants in any country. We spent decades straddling emigration, asylum, and exile on one side, and the numbing security of various documents—visas, residencies, citizenships—on the other. We had no plans. We still don't. But we've finally reached the stage where, having had our noses conclusively rubbed in impermanence, we have developed an appreciation for precarious positions. I think we might have something to say about what goes on inside black holes.

One of the pockets within this abyss is what is called "brain drain." This is actually an international space. When I first came to the U.S. as a foreign student in the 1970s I had a running joke with some fellow undergrad international students about starting a club called International Brain Drain Society. One night, after a few beers, a few of us even made little IBDS membership cards. Back then most members of IBDS would have been from the Third World—Africa, Asia, Latin America, the Middle East. (One can easily find long-lost friends in Roberto Bolaño or Agha Shahid Ali.) And after the fall of the Soviet Union we would have had to open our membership to the Eastern Bloc as well. By then more parts of the world were hemorrhaging brain than not. By now we would be taking in refugees from developed countries.

I dislike the phrase "brain drain" for two reasons. One, it implies that the countries that we left behind are now suffering from brain deficiency. That's ridiculous; brain is a renewable natural resource. Second, it implies that somehow the brains of emigrants are absorbed into the brain pool of the host countries. That's also ridiculous. Clearly our host countries are much more in need of cheap labor than brain—there's a surplus of the homegrown variety already. But, see, in our naivety we took our brains seriously.

The American husband of a relative of mine who lived in Iran for a few years in the late sixties told me this joke that circulated among the Americans in Iran at the time.

Question: What happens when all these Iranians who go to the U.S. to study stay there and never come back?
Answer: The average IQ of both countries is lowered.

I can just picture the various American "advisors" and tag-alongs passing on this joke under their breath at glittering dinner parties, holding large plates heaped with sumptuous Iranian food. I wish they had choked on those succulent pieces of kabab they were helping themselves to. But—suffering from an abundance of confidence—had we heard this joke back then we would more likely have dismissed it as American impudence than taken it to heart.

Years later I read a comment by Noam Chomsky that the intelligentsia of the Third World is naïve as to exactly how cynical western elites, including the intelligentsia, are. I agree. That's what I mean when I say that we took our brains too seriously. We took everybody's brains seriously, here, there, wherever. We thought there was inherent value in the gray matter. Many of us just did not get the message no matter how bluntly it was drummed into our heads: No submission, no prize.

The abyss into which my generation slid day by day in Iran was not all that different from the one we experienced outside. If our brains were chewed up and spat out in the west, theirs were spat out in virgin state.

But then again, there is something to be said for crude survival. Once I gave this topic to my freshman composition class in the Bronx: "An unexamined life is not worth living." One of my students put me to shame. "Any kind of life is worth living," she wrote. And as for us, the "burned generation" of more than one generation in Iran, we have perhaps now survived long enough to start crawling out of the black hole. It certainly seems the time has arrived to take a serious look inside the hole—heck, maybe even some of those celebrated gems might turn up, scattered near and far.

Or, as an American professor of mine put it less flatteringly years ago, as soon as the edge of a certain hostility dulls, Iranians will start crawling out of the woodwork in all kinds of places.

A bad case of asthma

The fact is that the days when Khanlari, Jafari, and Samimi were sent to jail now also belong to a "yesterday." Samimi of Offset can now be interviewed along with his post-revolution colleagues, though effort is made to disguise the singling out of the success of his tenure; the first volume of Jafari's book is published even if the second is held up in Ministry of Guidance; the memory of Khanlari is tolerated, if not exactly celebrated. But there is no end in sight to the price that is exacted from the brain that has not been drained from the country.

Bukhara is the name of a well-respected journal of arts and humanities that has been published for close to a decade. One of its most significant contributions has been the "evenings" it organizes to celebrate individual authors and artists. *Bozorgdasht* is a genre of public life that has a long history in Iran. It literally means "holding great" and is a gathering in honor of an accomplished individual, living or dead. It is just the kind of thing that the regime calls "exhumation." The publisher and editor of Bukhara battles daily to keep his journal and the bozorgdasht events going. He is singularly busy, calling his extra-prolific output "work therapy." I had not expected that he would have time to visit me, but he did. When I opened the door for him on the day of his visit he barely made it to the nearest seat, and collapsed into it with a severe asthma attack.

There are conditions in Iran beside which the fabled pollution of Tehran pales in ability to trigger asthma. He handed me an editorial from Keyhan, the extremist daily. "Exclusive

News," announced the title. "Iranian Artists' House has resumed its perverse activities." Iranian Artists' House is a popular gathering spot where many of Bukhara's bozorg-dasht evenings are held. The article boasted that as a result of "revelations" published in this newspaper the former director of the Artists' House had been replaced with one "approved" by the new mayor. It then went on to attack the most recent Bukhara Evening, a commemoration of the widely beloved poet Fereydoun Moshiri. Here is a quote from the editorial:

> "At this event court musicians from the period of *taghout* [derogatory word for the previous regime] praised the disgrace and prostitution of pre-revolution art. While many of the fasting audience members awaited a program in keeping with the stature of the holy month of Ramezan, Homayoun Khorram, a despicable figure of vulgar Iranian music, asked for a glass of water while delivering his speech."

Homayoun Khorram, a violinist and composer in his mid-seventies, is a national treasure.

> "The Artists' House proceeded to entertain the guests before the *azan* and *eftar*."

Not observing Ramezan is a serious charge but there are graver sins. The editorial went on:

> "During this event a letter by an escaped author was read in which the author mentioned his and Moshiri's collaboration with an intellectual who supported the massacre of people during the rule of the Shah. In this letter the author, on the pretext of recounting memories, paid respect to one of the advisors of Ashraf Pahlavi."

Ashraf Pahlavi is the twin sister of the Shah and the most vilified member of Pahlavi family. The "advisor" in question, I was informed, is Dr. Khanlari. Attributing an association with Ashraf Pahlavi is one of the highest forms of insult anyone can still think of. I suppose one can conclude that Khanlari is not yet dead enough for Keyhan. But attacks on people not at all dead are certainly more menacing.

> "The board of directors of the Artist's House has not yet disclosed the reasons behind its wide collaboration with a certain American spy and velvet-revolution strategist."

It is possible that the extremists in Iran are the only people who take a U.S. style "velvet revolution" seriously. The idea of American-led democratization insults the beliefs of some Iranians and the intelligence of all. Nevertheless, the charge of being connected to American plots, no matter how illusory the plot or the connection, is not to be taken lightly. The editorial finally narrowed in on its target:

> "There is cause for wonder that the editor of Bukhara, who is the link between Iranian press and the Israel Lobby in United States, has remained in his position."

Now, to be associated with the Israel Lobby is definitely worse than with Ashraf Pahlavi. In fact, compared to the Israel Lobby, Ashraf Pahlavi is almost quaint—so "yesterday." If I were the editor of Bukhara, I too would have an asthma attack.

The next night, sitting in the very spot where the editor had sat, it was the turn of an old friend of mine to pull something out of his briefcase. This friend probably holds a record for the number of NGOs he has started or worked with in Iran. He handed me an article he had downloaded from a news website with the title: "Enemies' Tactics against Religious Governance." It reported on the latest government position vis-à-vis NGOs. Here are some quotes from the article.

The speaker of the parliament: "One of the plans of our enemies is to make religious governance appear incompetent. Development of NGOs in Iran is a confrontational tactic and a weapon used against religious governance. The organizations that serve this goal must be identified."

Deputy Minister of Science: "Some NGOs are trying to channel our university students toward foreign intelligence centers so they can be used, or abused, for foreign interests at critical times."

Deputy Minister of Interior (a kinder, gentler approach): "Iranian NGOs must have reasonable expectations, more attuned to the circumstances of the country. Many of these organizations are not sufficiently familiar with the nature of certain domestic and international organizations and run into problems. A number of foreign countries have officially proclaimed their aim to bring about regime change in Iran, and towards that end are greedily eying certain NGOs. The Ministry of Interior wants to help these NGOs not to fall into this trap and to avoid problems."

And a word from a high-ranking member of the Revolutionary Guards: "Basij is the largest and most expansive NGO in the world." (The N in NGO be damned.)

The friend who showed me this article is an experienced observer of not just NGOs in Iran but the communities that are served by those organizations. He championed environmentalism before any of us had heard the word. He has hiked or driven to the most forgotten corners of the country, assessing environmental conditions, identifying needs and capabilities of communities, and collecting all kinds of material with high environmental, historical, social, and cultural value. He is knowledgeable and energetic, has street smarts and business savvy—and all his ventures, profit or nonprofit, inexplicably met with failure after the revolution. Longing to be active and needing a decent job, he finally relented a few years ago to being hired by a large foreign company whose only recommendation is that it is not American. It is one of the most powerful and aggressive of the many companies—owned by Iranians as well as non-Iranians—who are positioning themselves for the happy days of massive privatization right around the corner. My friend works for this company as a native nice guy, distributing the "external relations" resources at his disposal with generosity and good judgment. Though I am yet to learn the exact title of his position, it is safe to assume that the company is confident that it gets its money's worth out of a knowledgeable and savvy native like him.

His case demonstrates that sometimes when the brain doesn't go to the drain, the drain comes to the brain. It's called globalization.

The quote I cited above from the speaker of the parliament about the danger that NGOs pose for religious governance was taken from his speech at the inauguration of "Doctoral Programs at National Defense Universities." Whatever the nature of those programs or universities, the speaker's comments were a reminder that what is commonly called globalization is not the only global vision. Here is another quote from the speaker—and please note, "religious" is not intended to read "Islamic":

> "The need for religious governance is ever-increasing in the world today. Contrary to the strong opposition to this trend, the world is advancing in the direction of religious governance."

Those of us who don't have asthma gag.

Khayyam

My father loved Khayyam. The closer he got to death, and the more his lived and imagined lives mixed in his memory, the more he communed with two men: Khanlari, with whom he had studied and worked, and Khayyam.

My mother and I brought some of my dad's ashes to scatter in Iran. We wanted to pay his last tribute to the mountains where he had spent some of the happiest times of his life. We did not make a ceremony of it because he would have cringed at the idea.

Marjan drove us to the mountains. She is my oldest friend. We were friends as infants, like our brothers were before we came along. There is an ancient, preverbal bond between us—what I imagine "prehistoric" feels like. Having lost her father not too long ago, Marjan had just the right combination of personal experience and irreverence for the occasion. We chatted as she drove on new highways that were completely unknown to me. Our mothers talked quietly in the back seat.

I told her that in honor of my father's love for Khayyam I had half a mind to mix some of his ashes with pottery clay and make a cup. "Glaze it and drink vodka out of it—*tagari*," I said, partly joking.

We both thought about it for a minute. "I don't think one should drink out of one's parents" she finally said.

When we left the new highways behind and as the car climbed up the mountain road in low gear we caught sight of a beautiful white horse galloping ahead. In a minute there was an old pickup truck behind us with two guys hanging from its sides, gesticulating for us to pull over. We let them pass and in another minute they caught up with the tired horse. One of the men jumped down and with a little struggle managed to grab the horse by its mane and turn it back. We caught up with them and stopped. Marjan rolled down her window and I snapped some pictures. "Ran away from the stable..." explained the guy leading the horse past our car. As Marjan engaged him in her loopy prattle, the horse jerked its neck in a last attempt to break free. Its disheveled and sweaty gray mane glistened in the sun and its eyes flashed.

We picked a spot by a brook, overlooking a valley with a village on one side and a view of mountain peaks looking deceptively close on the other. It was a windy day. The wind snatched the ashes out of our hands before any reached the brook. It threw them back into our faces and dusted our clothes.

I mixed a pinch of ash with some dirt in my hand. I felt the gritty mixture of pebbles and bits of my father's bones on my palm. I suppose this is what I believe in. It's the only return there is.

My mother chose this Khayyam *roba'i* to send to friends with a picture of my father engrossed in reading a book:

> *I saw him astride the horse of earth—*
> *No blasphemy, no Islam, no religion, nor the world,*
> *No right, no truth, no law, and no certitude—*
> *Who in the two worlds has such gall?*

On being stuck

In 1987 I wrote about meeting with a professor of literature at Tehran University who smiled at my nationalist sentiments as he ignored hostile glances from his zealous quota students. Thoroughly well-versed in more than one literary tradition, this professor is a most versatile critic. He is also a significant contemporary poet. "Modernism is a tradition," he often reminds his students and readers. The word for tradition, *sonnat*, is the last word many of his students and readers, weary of Islamic regression, want to hear. What the supremacists of Islamic tradition make of this comment, I don't know.

I went to see this professor when I was in Tehran two years ago. We met at his office apartment where books don't just line the walls but are piled up high in rows on the floors. I wanted my husband to meet him and talk about a translation project but before we had a chance to settle into our conversation his doorbell rang. Catching sight of the visitors walking through the yard toward the living room, he remembered that he had made an appointment to see them before I had called. The visitors were a husband and wife, both former students of his. The woman, seamlessly clad in heavy black hejab, had just defended her dissertation and wanted to talk to the professor about publishing it. She still had that post-dissertation glow of relief though she was flushed with overheating under her dark synthetic layers and from her trip to Tehran from Qom.

When they walked into the room it was too late to change anything. I was sitting on the couch in short sleeves and uncovered hair. The fact that my husband was there of course eased things a bit; the husband after all does carry the final word. But we all knew that were there no husband at all, I would still be sitting in the same place dressed the same way. So we all ignored the awkwardness of our appearances and made polite conversation. After a good stretch of political chitchat the young woman's husband discreetly changed the subject to the purpose of his wife's visit.

Iranians are very tolerant of open disguise. The hejab is of course the best example of it. A considerable number of women wear it because they have to and everybody knows that the minute it is not forced on them, off it comes. Another trivial example is the non-alcoholic beer that became popular after the revolution. It was so much in demand in the early years that it was hard to find. Now it abundantly lines the shelves in sandwich shops. Everybody knows that it is a substitute for the real thing. The minute the ban on alcohol is lifted people will go back to drinking beer with their sandwiches. The same is true of watching prohibited films, listening to prohibited music, engaging in every kind of prohibited activity. We know; they know; the world knows.

We are sort of stuck in the roles we play. We can go neither forward nor backward. Oddly enough, while it is not hard to see that we are not going forward—role-playing is hardly the way toward a culture of honesty and openness—looking back is not as simple as it may seem. Here is an example.

A book about my grandparents has been stalled for some years now in the Ministry of Guidance (it is hard not to cringe every time I write the title of this governmental entity). My grandfather is a nationally recognized figure in education. There are, and were before the revolution, chapters about him in children's textbooks. But a book about even this state-sanctioned figure has proved problematic. We are told that this biography is not released on account of the photographs it contains of my grandparents and their various associates. My grandmother did not wear the veil—nor did any of the other women colleagues of my grandfather and certainly none of their offspring or students. What publishers routinely do to get old photographs published is to photoshop scarves onto women's heads and coverings onto their legs. Why these particular photographs have not cleared Guidance I don't know, but what is hard to get over, no matter how routine the practice, is putting hejab on the heads of long-deceased women. I am talking about painting scarves on the heads of women from a century ago. I hesitate to call it ironic—it's too ridiculous to be elevated to the rank of irony. I think it can best be described as being stuck. The book is stuck at the censors because the censors are stuck in their absurd procedures. And we are all frozen in the moment. We are not going forward and we can not even admit to our own past.

Taqi Jafari writes that after kashf-e hejab his mother's veil was torn off her head one day in the street. He later found her in bed, delirious with fever from the shock. He also writes that it was after kashf-e hejab that women started working at different jobs, including some in print-houses. Reading the account of Jafari's mother and grandmother cooped up alone in a dank room, spinning thread in semi-darkness, I can't help wondering whether they would have preferred working in a printshop. Even hard labor is easier when there is camaraderie and option. Jafari proved that grueling as labor in turn-of-the-twentieth-century printshops was, it did not have to be a dead end. I can't help thinking that his mother, adamantly religious as she was, would have opted for that work rather than the mind-numbing labor that was her lot. There's no question that printshops paid far better. What's more, if she wanted to educate her son so badly, would she have refused a little education for herself?

The Islamic Republic never took away the right of women to go to school. Nor did it oppose the right of women to work, though it did impose restrictions and ceilings on it. It certainly did not take away women's right to vote. In fact, the Republic is modern enough to pride itself on the growing number of Iranian women in higher education and various professions as well as their participation in elections. This liberal stance was far from the Islamist agenda in the past. The generation of women who are being photoshopped into

Islamic garb today fought the religious establishment a century ago for the right to send their daughters to school. Khomeini himself bitterly fought against women's right to vote before he was exiled in 1964. But would the Islamic Republic ever admit that its own progressive policies of today are owed to the rights and freedoms women won in clear opposition to the Islamic establishments of the time?

Does that heavily-veiled recent PhD really prefer sweating under her layers of black in the summer heat to wearing something more appropriate to the climate?

I am certainly not going to budge from my position vis-à-vis the Islamic Republic's dress code, hence the openness of my disguise. I wonder if the veiled graduate was also in some kind of disguise. Back when women lived in seclusion behind closed doors and layers of cloth, the only trips they made were to the public baths. They did not commute to Tehran to work on PhDs. Can this educated woman not be aware of what won her the right to pursue a PhD? Is this absurd veiling a denial of that history or is it a form of disguise that people of my ideological persuasion are not registering? Or is she just stuck?

The first week of the month of *Mehr*, the beginning of autumn, is celebrated every year as the Week of Sacred Defense. It memorializes Saddam Hossein's attack on Iran in 1980 and the eight-year war that followed. This year the ubiquitous official banners and posters of the "Week," hanging from every lamppost and pasted on every wall, posed a very important question: "What would have happened if we had not resisted?" The U.S. in its various alliances has waged a war on Iran at least since the revolution and the Islamic Republic has defended the country. Even the staunchest critics of the regime have to admit that it has earned the right to ask this question.

The word I'm translating as "resistance" is *istadegi*. It implies not just the act of resistance but perseverance in holding the stance. It is an excellent description of a position Iranians of all kinds of political and ideological persuasions have held for as long as we remember. It is a posture we have maintained for so long that we have become collectively and individually immobilized in it. Sometimes it feels like conflicting pressure from all sides is what holds us up.

When the American hostages were taken in 1979, in response to the affront I suffered from American acquaintances I came up with a clever little witticism. It went like this: "There are two stages to American foreign policy—crime and prejudice followed by pride and punishment." The crime and prejudice phase is at work while the U.S. goes unchallenged in its sense of entitlement and supremacy over other nations, and pride and punishment kick in once those people presume to assert their sovereignty. (The 1979 revolution was a declaration of independence of sorts: "When in the course of human events it becomes necessary for one people to dissolve the political bonds which have connected them with another...") For the past three decades a lot of Iranians have had to quietly put up a double resistance: against the punishment and derision of injured American pride on the one hand, and against all that is wrong in Iran on the other.

The question of what would have happened if we had not maintained our *istadegi* is excellent in many respects. For one thing, because it touches on a predicament that many Iranians share, it has a unifying effect. For another, it sends a message in response to the increasingly belligerent American rhetoric. Iran is a bold country. It has now suffered decades of American punishment and it remains bold. Can the United States really expect the nation to just whimper and give in? Or can any Iranian, for or in opposition to the Islamic Republic, support any action whose impetus bears disdain for our national sovereignty?

This stubborn independence is rooted partly in the pride and confidence of an old people and partly in a few centuries of battling colonial powers. Imperial Russia and the British in India were our neighbors. Every ruinous treaty and outrageous concession they imposed on Iran met with opposition. From the Shah's harem women boycotting tobacco on account of the British concession, to the mob induced to slaughter the Russian dandy Griboedov in revenge for the catastrophic treaty he had negotiated, a wide range of people have fought foreign imperial designs. We studied the history of this resistance in school and lived through the defiance against replacement of old British and Russian colonial interests by new American ones. And it cannot be denied that the clergy were an important part of this fight. As late as the 1960s, the Status of Forces Agreement imposed by the Americans on the Shah was seen as the revival of old colonialist Capitulation laws and deeply despised. It was Khomeini's leadership of the opposition to the American SOFA that led to his exile in 1964.

For centuries now, significant numbers of Iranians, regardless of political or ideological affiliation, have operated in resistance mode. Everyone has been fighting for sovereignty. And where indeed would we be if we hadn't resisted? This is not just a legitimate question but could very well serve as a rhetorical point of departure for writing the history of modern Iran. It can be asked of anyone. Where would the Islamic Republic be if it had not resisted Saddam? Where would the country be? Where would the opposition be if it had not resisted in jail under the Shah and later under the Islamic Republic? Where would women be if they had not resisted the denial of their history and their rights? Where would we exiles be if we had not resisted our double bind? Where would the victorious be and where would the defeated be? Where would Khomeini and his legacy be? And, even, where would the Shah—and his father, for that matter—have been if they had not put up their share of resistance along the way?

We are all defined by our resistance. And we are stuck.

Last night at Darakeh

My friend Reza has the kind of eccentric mind that can make something fresh out of things you think you wrote off a long time ago. He is the very opposite of smugness. When I was an impressionable teenager and he no more than in his early twenties, he made me see the smugness in a lot of people I looked up to. Awareness of that one quality saved me from making some major mistakes, such as joining one of the various radical leftist groups like many of my friends. Who knows from what horrors Reza's influence spared me and my family. Now I use him to check elements of smugness in myself.

He has always been one of my best friends and over the years I have become increasingly enamored of his wife Sheri. They both used to work at the old National Radio and Television and have interesting stories of what took place in the country's largest media entity during the revolution. For many years, after Reza's position was "cleansed" of his person, Sheri supported their family. I remember eating dinner with them on a cloth spread on the floor in a dark corner of their apartment during the war with Iraq, a habit that stayed with them even after the bombardments were over. Their children were small, life was dangerous and livelihood uncertain, but they were happy.

Sheri is the kind of woman who disappears into the kitchen and emerges with a glass of fresh-squeezed sweet lemon juice (because you have a cold) without missing a word of the conversation. She is sweet and kind and sharp—and she has no trouble standing her own ground. In fact, she is quite ingenious in the ways she does that.

Two years ago when I saw Reza and Sheri it was right after the presidential elections. They told me how Reza was approached by one of the candidates to make a documentary film for his campaign. This particular hard-line candidate had bailed Reza out of a precarious situation in the past and felt that he was owed a favor. He would not accept Reza politely declining and was anxious to prove what an attractive candidate he was. While Reza was sweating bullets over what to do, Sheri issued her ultimatum that if he took this project she would leave him. "But he doesn't accept my refusal," Reza pleaded. "Leave it to me then," said Sheri. "I'll make sure he gets the message."

Getting chummy with Reza, the candidate invited himself to dinner at their house. "Just some bread and cheese with the family," he said. "Please don't let your wife go to any trouble." This is where Sheri took matters into her hands. It would be an exceedingly formal affair, she decided. She went out and paid a lot of money for a few kilos of the largest shrimps she could find. She took a lot of trouble cleaning them (something she hates) and made a nice presentation of them as the main attraction of the multi-course dinner. Now, in Islamic diet, shrimp is a *mobah* food—*halal* is food that is okay to eat, *haram* is forbidden, and *mobah* is that which is not entirely forbidden but is certainly not recommended. No self-respecting hard-liner eats shrimp. On the other hand, preparing the most expensive and labor-intensive food for your guests is the highest display of formal respect. When this presidential candidate was called to the dinner table he found himself faced with a huge platter of shrimp meticulously prepared and prominently displayed, and the lady of the house presiding at the table without hejab. He must have gasped! "I do as I want in my own house and I hadn't invited him," Sheri explained to me.

The guy of course did not touch the shrimp and the edge of his chumminess quickly wore off. Getting the point that no collaboration was really possible between Reza and his campaign, he cut short his after-dinner stay. Meanwhile, Reza and Sheri awaited some form of retort before he left. It finally came in the form of what to him must have been the ultimate insult to any woman. "Women of a certain age don't really need to wear the hejab," he casually remarked. "The hejab is only for young and attractive women."

Thirty years ago when Khomeini took a swipe at Oriana Fallaci with a similar remark, Sheri and I were young and not bad looking. I can say with confidence that we were far from flattered to qualify as such in the Imam's eyes. We did not see the hejab as affirmation of our youth and beauty nor feel that not wearing it made us any less off limits. What we saw in Khomeini's outburst was a pitiful rage. It was an admission of his inability to engage a woman on the level that she was engaging him and his frustration at failing to impose his will on her—to have his way with her, so to speak. The same thing happened with this candidate. He was not able to impose himself to the extent he wished. In a certain battle with Sheri and Reza he must have felt that he had run out of ammo—or as we say in Persian, his spatula must have hit the bottom of the pot.

Or shall we call it impotent rage?

As far as my friends were concerned, it was a small price to pay for freedom from the torment of an obligation and a disagreeable association. Be that as it may, I wonder if we might be able to turn the situation into a win-win for all concerned. I wonder if it would be possible for women past an official cut-off age to sign a document certifying that they can live without being the object of a particular kind of attention. Could then some of us at least end this hejab masquerade?

But alas, not yet.

My last night in Tehran I went to Darakeh again, this time with Reza and Sheri. Eating a bubbling *dizi* with freshly baked bread under the stars and the waning moon of Ramezan was the best ending I could think of for my trip. It was a clear moonlit night and the chill of the mountains in October was making itself felt. We huddled cross-legged around our platter of food wishing for the warmth of one of those electric *qalyoun* warmers. But we couldn't have one. Since my last evening at Darakeh the restaurant had been shut down on account of serving water-pipes to women. (Smoke, Don't smoke.) There were no drinks or pickles or any kind of side dishes either. "We were suddenly given permission to reopen and we didn't have time to replenish our stock," our waiter explained.

The night I had been in this restaurant with Marjan it was a hopping place with lots of people grouped around food and tea and qalyoun. It had definitely been a different scene. When Marjan and I left rather late that night people were still streaming in. "I was born in Finland and now I wait tables in Iran," a fair-haired young waiter was joking with some customers. Out on the street we flipped through cinema magazines and others I hadn't heard of. We sauntered leisurely toward our car.

On the edge of the busiest part of the strip we suddenly came across a makeshift table covered with series of pamphlets under the general title "Civil Rights." Three young men were manning the table, one of whom, a slick and smooth-talking "communications and public relations major," was clearly the leader. The other two mostly looked nervously around. I thought at first that they were with one of those NGOs that the government is so suspicious of, but I was wrong. The pamphlets were produced by "Deputy of Judicial Training," a bona fide branch of the Judiciary of the Islamic Republic. There was one publication, "Aware Citizen," that was jointly produced with UNDP. The young men charged us a nominal fee for the pamphlets because they said people are more likely to read something they have paid for.

"This is part of a project to acquaint people with the constitution," said the assertive young man. "If we want the rule of law, people need to know the laws." He even went so far as to suggest that if we want to change the constitution we need to first acquaint ourselves with the existing one. He drew my attention to one pamphlet discussing the legal framework for fighting "Illegal Detentions." (I must have looked to him like the kind who would or should be concerned about that sort of thing.) I picked up pamphlets about laws concerning women and children: marriage, divorce, custody of children, remarriage, adoption. There was one spelling out the laws governing punishment for the killing of women by men, which is half as severe as punishment for the killing of men by men—the crudest demonstration of what people call gender apartheid. Just too crude.

Who could argue with legal education? Who could argue with building "civil society"? Who would take issue with collaboration between Iranian judiciary and UNDP? Who doesn't need to learn about HIV and SMS, MMS and EMS offenses—that is, offenses committed through the use of Short Message Service, Multimedia Message Service, and Enhanced Message Service? Who would argue against using quotes from the prophet to urge people to behave towards each other in a friendly manner?

In 1919, the last prime minister of Ahmad Shah Qajar signed a treaty that turned Iran into a "protectorate" of the British Empire. Mohammad Ali Foroughi, a seasoned diplomat opposed to this treaty, was removed from his sphere of influence by being sent to the Paris Peace Conference and all but abandoned there. "Iran has neither government nor nation," he mused in a letter he wrote during his semi-exile and which was widely distributed in Iran. Foroughi himself subsequently chose to build a government through Reza Shah and his new Pahlavi dynasty. But building a "nation" is a more complicated matter. In 1919, Touran Mirhadi's parents left Europe for Iran, Khanlari began elementary school, and Taqi Jafari was born. It is people like these who undertook to build the nation. And at any rate, as far as I'm concerned, the kind of nation envisioned by people like these is the only kind of nation worth building—or belonging to.

I had no arguments with the civil rights spread at Darakeh. I just didn't like that slick PR major peddling the rule of law and civil rights like so much corporate ware. And I couldn't understand why his buddies seemed so uncomfortable and nervous. They looked out of place and under some kind of constraint. I could better picture them among those unnamed young Iranians displaying their eye-popping talents on YouTube, or imagine them as the faces behind those rapid-fire blogs whose sarcasm alone is highly corrosive. It is deeply satisfying how the anonymity of the internet both shields and gives exposure to Iranian youth.

None of this was going on my last night at Darakeh. The whole area was quiet and seemed depressed. Reza and Sheri and I just talked together.

I never tire of hearing personal accounts of the days of the revolution. It is always surprising and revealing to hear how people act when so many restraints are suddenly removed. It was certainly the excitement of a lifetime. Criss-crossing the city on foot, carrying on political discussions at the top of your lungs, toting looted guns, strewing flowers, piling up in cars to see more of what is going on, smiling broadly at strangers, sleeping with the radio on, distributing sweets, calling friends... The days were very full. I missed all that and my friends always oblige me with their accounts of those days. And there are always new things to learn—like which media celebrities joined in barricading the National Radio and Television building against the Shah's soldiers, only to be later excommunicated or assassinated in exile.

One of my last memories of Iran before the revolution was another night spent with Reza and Sheri. A mutual bookstore friend and I went to their apartment for dinner. Martial law had just been declared in Tehran and having missed the curfew deadline we ended up spending the night there. As the hours wore on and we tired of our excited conversation, we leaned against the bolsters on the floor and watched Reza and Sheri's sleeping baby. A little gold *vanyakad* prayer was pinned to his shirt. "All you want to do is to protect your child," said Reza. "You will even give superstition a chance."

It was a balmy night. The windows were flung open and the sheer curtains billowed in the breeze. We listened to the sounds of enforced curfew outside. "Stop," we heard shouts from the soldiers. "You. Stop." We listened to the gunshots in silence. It was difficult to make out who was shooting whom. It was even more difficult to know what to feel.

On this last night at Darakeh we climbed the muddy stairs of the restaurant back to street level. We were quiet.

"How they have tormented us all these years," Reza sighed. "They are tormenting us still."

Hafez

Wonder not at the revolution of the times
For the wheel has of these tales
thousands and thousands in memory

When all else fails, Iranians take refuge in Hafez. This is probably the single most Iranian practice since the 14th century.

Hafez is revered more than any other poet. There is national consensus that he has achieved an almost impossible pinnacle in both poetry and thought. The greatest scholars are judged by their understanding of Hafez and there is more commentary written on his poetry than on any other. No serious musician, stricly classical or riotously contemporary, can resist the challenge of interpreting Hafez. But it should not be supposed that Hafez belongs to the lofty realms of the hyper-educated or brilliantly accomplished: A great number of people know his poetry by heart without understanding all the words or even being able to read. One of the reasons that there is no definitive edition of Hafez is that the poems were preserved as much in memory as in written form.

The unique place of Hafez in Persian literature has earned him somewhat of a divine status. He is called "voice of the unseen" and "interpreter of mysteries," and the book of his poems, his *divan,* is quite regularly used for divination. It is common to make a wish, or pose a problem, and open the divan at random to read the ghazal for the poet's guidance. It is not an exaggeration to say that many an important decision is still made in such consultation with Hafez. There are people who make a living interpreting him for lay folks and many more who sell ghazals on the streets packaged like surprise trinkets in identical wrappings. Some peddlers have trained parakeets who pluck the right poem for you from a pack of indistinguishable envelopes. As for the question of divinity, one could say Hafez plays on a divine playing field. He himself claimed that his poetry adorns heaven and that angels spend their time memorizing it.

It is certainly the case that in many houses the divan of Hafez either replaces or complements the Koran at official ceremonies. Like the Koran, this is a text that is lived more than it is read. But if the former has relied on a great deal of might and method to find its way into people's lives, the latter has achieved it on merit alone. In fact, over the centuries a subtle competition has developed between the Koran, the "miracle" of Islam, and the divan of Hafez. The idea of elevating a text to the status of a miracle is one of the more intriguing aspects of Islam, and in Iran the possibility of making this kind of elevation has been extended to Hafez. While the blasphemy of calling his divan a downright miracle has never been openly committed, his poetry comes close to being received as miracle. Unlike the Koran which must be recited in Arabic, however, the poetry of Hafez is exquisite composition in a language Persian-speakers understand, and if there is a miraculous quality to this poetry, it is its sublime combination of the exalted and the intimate. In fact, a defining characteristic of the ghazals is that they can be read on multiple levels, from the most mundane and profane to heights and depths that cross over to what is called sacred. Hafez was not bashful about expressing his supreme confidence in the excellence of his poetry—he frequently used the convention of citing his own name in the last line of a ghazal to do so—but he himself made no supernatural claims.

Hafez was not at all the sort to get caught up in orthodoxy or sanctimony of any kind. Although he was vastly educated in Arabic and the Koran ("Hafez" means someone who knows the whole Koran by heart) his secularism is the stuff of national legend. A great deal of his poetry is a sometimes subtle, sometimes blunt debunking of religiosity, though God and Koranic (not to mention Old and New Testament) allusions have their place in his vast poetic landscape. It is the complexity of this landscape that allows his poetry to be interpreted on so many different levels. It is even possible, contrary to the customary pseudo-mysticism that is attached to him (especially in translation), to read Hafez on the level of not only the cut-and-dried historical but the decidedly political. His iconoclasm was very much the result of the times in which he lived—a period similar in many ways to the recent past.

Hafez lived at a turbulent time between the two Mongol invasions of Iran, Genghis Khan in the 13th century and Tamerlane in the 14th. In his lifetime, his native city of Shiraz was ruled by two dynasties and at least six rulers. Early in his career Hafez enjoyed the friendship and patronage of the last Shah of the Inju dynasty, during whose reign—great political turmoil aside—the city of Shiraz enjoyed a good deal of social freedom. The open pursuit of pleasure was a way of life of which both the literati and the Shah partook. Perhaps the precariousness of the period made escapes into the abandon of the moment more appealing.

Those relatively free days came to an end when the Inju dynasty was toppled and Hafez's patron murdered by Mobarezeddin Mohammd of the Mozaffarid dynasty. Amir Mobarez, as he was commonly known, was a puritanical and savage ruler who installed a brutal religious order in Shiraz to wipe out what he saw as the licentious rule of his predecessor. He certainly practiced what he preached. He was known to momentarily interrupt his reading of the Koran to slice someone's head off. He boasted to his son that he had personally executed "seven or eight hundred" men. Hafez recorded the reign of Amir Mobarez as a dark and ominous time: taverns were closed, pleasure punished, love outlawed, and thinkers terrorized. Inevitably, hypocrisy ruled the land. Hafez pursued his way of life, wrote, and communicated with other poets, all while under the menacing shadow of Amir Mobarez and his men. Hafez's defiance of false piety and his abhorrence of the hypocricy that was unleashed on his city was openly expressed in his poetry.

> *Drink wine, Hafez, and seek pleasure*
> *But do not like others*
>   *turn the Koran into a snare of deceit*

Amir Mobarez was eventually deposed and blinded by his own son, Shah Shoja. The young shah was a man of letters, a bon-vivant, and an admirer of Hafez. (A poet of some merit himself, he presumed to critique Hafez.) Though he overturned his father's puritanical rule and returned some ease to Shiraz, Shah Shoja was a volatile sort and had his phase of puritanical lapse. He is the one, however, credited with attaching the famous label of *mohtaseb* to his father. The persona of the *mohtaseb*, the ostensibly pious and gleefully brutal enforcer of public morality, appears frequently in Hafez. And the face that is revealed is more than merely ascetic.

> *Do not drink with the city's mohtaseb, Hafez*
> *For he drinks your wine and casts rocks at the cup*

While enjoying the free life restored by Shah Shoja, Hafez maintained a cordial but guarded relationship with him. The lines of praise on whose composition his livelihood depended were never overdone, quite legitimate, and always brilliant. While at times Hafez wrote with some personal affection for the young shah, he was aware that the "renaissance prince" was prince foremost. Shah Shoja was in perpetual bloody conflict with his brothers, ended up blinding his own son, and most brutally murdered a vazir who was a long-time mentor of Hafez. The longing of the great poet's soul was sometimes simply for freedom from the burden of dependence.

> *The glad moment when in drunken self-sufficiency*
> *I am liberated from both Shah and Vazir*

Kashf-e Hejab

The dark cloud of puritanical violence never entirely lifted under Shah Shoja. The terror of the times of Amir Mobarez continued its threat of comeback. Hafez did not just fear the consequences of the reign of the pious but his intelligence was insulted by it.

> *How long, zahed, will you deceive me like a child*
> *With apples from the garden and milk and honey*

Zahed means "ascetic." It is another word, like *mohtaseb*, that is used throughout the ghazals of Hafez, referring to the sanctimonious guardians of morality who stop short of no brutality in holding on to whatever it is that is the real source of their power.

It is tempting to draw parallels between the fate of Amir Mobarez and the mohtaseb and zahed of our time. Perhaps today too mohtaseb *père* has reason to fear blinding at the hands of mohtaseb *fils*—regardless of the question of puritanism. Then again, maybe today the dispute will be settled in the family more amicably. The sure thing is that, just as in the 14th century, there is no threat from any domestic source outside the dynasty. One can even extend the analogy to the invasion of Tamerlane. While the Mozaffarid princes were blinding each other as they alternately drank themselves into oblivion or enforced religion, Tamlerlane was laying siege to city after city until he finally arrived at the gates of Shiraz. But it is too unsettling to carry the analogy this far. What it forebodes is the invasion of the country by an empire-building foreign army. Luckily for Hafez that happened toward the end of his life.

There is one important difference between now and the 14th century, however. The zahed and mohtaseb of our time are far from unacquainted with Hafez and are themselves—no less than any other Iranian—products of seven hundred years of his influence. Khomeini wrote ghazals that were passable in quality (replete with wine and lover imagery) and certainly literate. Khamenei is known to be quite a cultivated man and

Khatami certainly looks it. Ahmadinejad is far from illiterate himself—and on and on. In fact, I would bet that not a single obscure member of basij, revolutionary guards, or an official in any capacity in the Islamic Republic—any one who takes his religion seriously—can be found in whose brain there is no synaptic activity in response to Hafez.

My idea of justice is to bring these men to face Hafez.

> *Begone*
> *   you self-absorbed zahed*
> *For from my eyes and yours*
> *   the mystery beyond this screen*
> *   is concealed and will remain concealed*

Hafez is able to take his readers—zahed and mohtaseb included—by the hand and lead them to a place that is better for everybody. We would perhaps do well to trust his judgement that even the self-absorbed zahed and their henchmen stand a chance of being humbled by what cannot be known. It brings to my mind Khanlari inviting the revolutionary guards to read with him in his study, guns laid down against stacks of books... Justice is fiction.

Tackling the mystery beyond the screen, what lies just beyond perception, is what has earned Hafez the epithet of "voice of the unseen"—or more literally, "mouthpiece from the invisible." There are a number of words in Hafez that refer to that critical layer that conceals something very important, something that is almost palpable but ultimately beyond our full grasp. These words can be translated as "drape," "mask," "curtain," "cloak," "screen," and while subtly nuanced they are almost interchangeable. A prominent one on the list is "hejab"—the veil.

> *The dust of my body*
> *   is the hejab on the face of my being.*
> *Happy the moment I throw the drape from that face*

The body revealing its true face as the dust that it is, is the "passion" according to a great deal of Persian poetry; it lies at the intersection of poetry and mysticiscm. The longing for the shedding of that final hejab is not unique to Hafez. There is a great deal of powerful poetry in Persian that can, especially in combination with music, induce a trance that simulates the experience of that moment of freedom. But this kind of exhiliration is momentary and there remains quite a distance to travel between now and that final kashf-e hejab. There are many covers to take, faces to hide, and masks to don between now and then. Hafez was quite conscious of this. His suffering of the perils and compromises of patronage is not lost on his readers, and his use of poetic devices (*iham*, for instance) to maintain his distance from the intrigues of his patrons is ingenious. He was never far from the necessity of hiding behind layers of concealment and he knew from experience that no hejab is free of deception.

> *Pass the wine—for if you look closely,*
> *the pious, the holy, the mohtaseb and Hafez*
> *All engage in deception*

Guises and disguises, falsehoods and false fronts have indistinguishably mingled in Iran for as long as any one can remember. Camouflage has become part of our genetic makeup. Incongruent conciliation and tenacious contradiction are the natural order of things. Change occurs despite itself. Politically, Iran is a paradox.

The women's movement in Iran speaks of the day when our laws will catch up with our culture. This is inevitable. "Law," no matter how savagely enforced, is no match for how people choose to live their lives and what they will wrest from restriction. While we are still grappling with the question "How in the world did this happen to us...?" circumstances themselves change. This time around, the shedding of grotesquely backward laws and cumbersome garments will probably take place with a great deal more ease than Mohammad

Reza's Shah's reforms or Reza Shah's kashf-e hejab. The word kashf means revelation. A century ago "revelation" evoked the idea of political awakening in general as well as its particular application to the rights of women. But that is not necessary anymore: People, not least women, cannot be any more politically awake. The more tenacious hejabs of today are not those that cover women's bodies but those that conceal true faces. One important face, that of Islam itself, lies beneath the mask of "cultural revolution."

The Islamic Republic has always spoken proudly of its cultural revolution, without a hint of irony or apparent awareness of the negative associations of the phrase. But this can change. A great deal of what has passed for Islam in the past thirty years is an Islamic-flavored fabrication—part manufactured culture, part traditions distorted by amplification and by the force with which they are imposed. The most informed critique of this comes from the more authentic culture of Islam. What is called "traditional Islam" in Iran is perhaps best positioned to expose the disingenuousness that has passed for Islam in the past thirty years. Authenticity is after all the only answer to cultural revolution.

With the shedding of masks and veils a great many new faces emerge. This is a prospect to look forward to. Much of it, like the manuscripts awaiting publication, has already taken form and bides its time under the increasingly thin layer that separates underground life from the open. A great deal more will pop up with the urgency of released pressure. We will undoubtedly witness an explosion of revelations.

But then again, the peeling of layer after layer of concealment and mask and the painstaking generation of multiplicities of faces and aspects is a daunting prospect. Relief in the form of abandoning the undertaking certainly beckons. And there is always the threat of running out of time... So, one may well conclude, Why this frantic exertion—pass the wine—Hafez has said it all.

Hafez has transcended it all. The shedding of hejabs, masks, disguises, and deceit is compelling only up to a point.

And the final liberation from the dust of the body is inevitable and indeed the fate of us all—there's no need to rush it and there is always trance for experiential indulgence. The satisfaction that a great man like Hafez seeks is of a different order. The peaks that he climbs are far from attainable by all.

> *None stripped the mask from the face of thought*
> *like Hafez*

Hafez writes from the threshold of illumination just on the other side of perception and thought. It is a paradoxically secular vantage point. That famous physicist who imagined himself traveling with a beam of light would understand. Imagine the poetry that would emerge from that joy ride. This is *kashf-e hejab* of the highest order.

As for Iranian women, there is nothing to overcome. We shall overwhelm.

And it would be good to remember that if there are irrepressible women in Iran, there are also men who have expected no less all along. So many of us, women and men, have had enough of this resurrection of the ruinous ways of seven centuries ago. *Ma ra bas,* the refrain from one of the most glorious ghazals of Hafez, is perhaps our best rallying cry: *Enough!*

There will be a renaissance this time too—or rather, the renaissance will surface from underground. What will in the end overwhelm the ugliness and brutality—the illness—that has dominated the country for the past thirty years is intelligence, art, and endurance. It has been done before.

> *It is recorded in the chronicle of the world*
> *Our lasting*

It may have been our bad luck to relive the nightmare of the times of Hafez but it is certainly our good fortune to still speak his language.

Printed in the United States
139598LV00002B/1/P